The Body Coach Series

Core Strength

**Build Your Strongest Body Ever
with Australia's Body Coach®**

Paul Collins

Meyer & Meyer Sport

British Library Cataloguing in Publication Data
A catalogue record for this book is available from the British Library

Paul Collins
Core Strength
Maidenhead: Meyer & Meyer Sport (UK) Ltd., 2009
ISBN 978-1-84126-249-9

© 2009 by Paul Collins (text & photos)
and Meyer & Meyer Sport (UK) Ltd. (Layout)
Aachen, Adelaide, Auckland, Budapest, Cape Town, Graz, Indianapolis,
Maidenhead, New York, Olten (CH), Singapore, Toronto

Member of the World
Sport Publishers' Association (WSPA)
www.w-s-p-a.org

Printed and bound by: B.O.S.S Druck und Medien GmbH, Germany
ISBN 978-1-84126-249-9
E-Mail: verlag@m-m-sports.com
www.m-m-sports.com

Core Strength

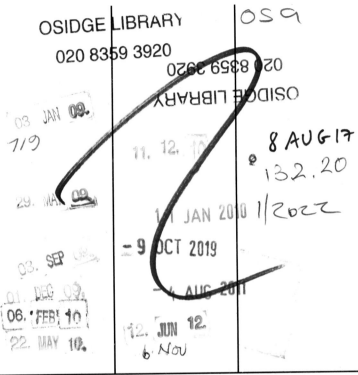

Please return/renew this item by the
last date shown to avoid a charge.
Books may also be renewed by phone
and Internet. May not be renewed if
required by another reader.

www.libraries.barnet.gov.uk

BARNET
LONDON BOROUGH

Acknowledgements

I would like to thank the following people in the development of this book: Alex Coombes, Alicia King, Ben Austin, Clayton Kearney, James Beasley, Lara Davenport, Cameron Delaney, Melissa Mitchell, Fiona Warneke, Pat Daley, Jon Bell, Narelle Simpson, Graeme (Grub) Carroll, Henson Family, George Lazarou, Ron Palmer, Dean Landy, Nigel Rowden, Paul Bulato, Dr Daniel Magee, Dr Nathan Gibbs, Jeff Pross (Physio), Dr Michael Hubbard (Osteopath). Geoff Spice, Daniel Spice, Wayne McDonald, Narelle Diamond, Howard Wells, Luke Jurcevic, Garry Rush, Amanda Cartaar, Linda Collins and my family for their ongoing support.

Medical Disclaimer:
The exercises and advice given in this book are in no way intended as a substitute for medical advice and guidance. It is sold with the understanding that the author and publisher are not engaged in rendering medical advice. Because of the differences from individual to individual, your doctor and physical therapist should be consulted to assess whether these exercises are safe for you. Always consult your doctor and physical therapist before starting this or any other exercise program. The author and publisher will not accept responsibility for injury or damage occasioned to any person as a result of participation, directly or indirectly, of the use and application of any of the contents of this book.

Contents

Note: Body Coach®, The Body Coach®, Belly Busters®, Thigh Busters®, 3 Hour Rule®, Fastfeet®, Quickfeet®, Posturefit®, Speedhoop®, The Body for Success™, Collins-Technique™, Collins Lateral Fly™, LumbAtube™, Spinal Unloading Block®; Rebound Medicine Ball™, 3B's Principle™, Abs Only™ Class, Body Bell™, Collins Rotations™ and Australia's Personal Trainer™ are all trademarks of Paul Collins.

Introduction

Welcome!

I'm The Body Coach, Paul Collins your exclusive personal coach here to guide and motivate you towards building your strongest body ever using your own body weight. A major breakthrough in exercising, *Core Strength* provides practical hands-on training with body weight exercises for every major muscle group including the use of Pilates based principles. What's more, core strength training is a substitute for lifting heavy weights. And, that's just part of the story.

The body weight exercises prescribed are the exact ones I have used to train the first-timer just starting out in exercise, right through to world-class athletes. Exercises themselves include the use of affordable equipment that challenges the body such as:

- Fitness Balls
- Medicine Balls
- Resistance Bands
- Hand Weights

For the lay person *Core Strength* helps in the development of better posture, body awareness and joint stability. Whereas for the athlete and coach it provides the capabilities for improving athletic performance. The exercises themselves aim to tone and strengthen muscles for better shape and definition. One of the major benefits is that these exercises can be performed anytime, anywhere by all age groups and ability levels including kids, adults, athletes and fitness enthusiasts alike. *Core Strength* is also an educational tool to assist coaches and teachers alike in developing ongoing training programs for keeping their athletes and teams fit, strong and healthy all year round.

Packed with over 100 exercises to choose from, each chapter targets body weight exercises for different muscle groups, including the abdominal muscles and lower back, chest and arms, back and arms, shoulders, legs and hip regions. The finer details of each exercise is promoted through the introduction of the revolutionary Collins Technique™, which aims to bring balance back into the muscles by developing a synergistic energy flow throughout the body. At the end of each chapter, these exercises have been summarized with space available to record the number of repetitions and set to perform. It also includes a resistance band rotator cuff strengthening program and series of Core Strength Training Routines for the following:

- Post-Pregnancy
- Running
- Racquet & Bat Sports
- Ball Sports
- Balance Sports
- Swimming
- Golf
- Kids

As you will discover all exercises form part of a core strength continuum that allows everyone from the first time exerciser right through to world-class athletes to be challenged. You also have the opportunity to test your current core-strength to see where you stand and how you are progressing. Whether you are reading this text as a coach, competitive or recreational athlete or fitness enthusiast, I hope it will encourage you to learn more about your body and the benefits of core strength training using your own body weight. Most importantly, you now have a program of exercises within easy reach that will help keep your body strong, muscles toned and confidence high.

I look forward to working with you!

www.thebodycoach.com

About the Author

Paul Collins is an Award-winning Personal Trainer in Australia and prolific author and presenter on fitness and weight loss topics.

Each year Paul inspires tens of thousands of people through appearances on TV, radio, print media and seminars. Coaching since age 14, Paul has personally trained world-class athletes and teams in a variety of sports from athletics through to rugby league, soccer, squash, tennis and many others including members of the Australian Olympic Swimming Team. He is also a key presenter to the Australian Track and Field Coaching Association, Australia Swimming Coaches and Teachers Association, NSW Squash Academy, Australian Karate Team and the Australian Fitness Industry.

Paul is an outstanding athlete in his own right, having played grade level in the national rugby league. He is also a former Australian Budokan Karate Champion, A-grade Squash Player and NSW Masters Athletics Track & Field State Champion.

As a leader in the field of personal fitness and weight loss, Paul has successfully combined a sports fitness background with a Bachelor of Physical Education Degree and international certification as a Strength and Conditioning Coach and Personal Trainer. As designer of The Body Coach® book and DVD series, exercise products and educational programs, Paul travels internationally to present a highly entertaining series of corporate Health & Well-being Seminars.

Paul's goal is to help people get fit, lose weight, look good and feel great!

For more details visit: www.thebodycoach.com

Chapter 1

Core Strength with the Collins-Technique™

The Collins-Technique™ supplements cardiovascular training (heart and lung fitness) by introducing a new era of core strength training that focuses on improving body awareness and muscle tone. Knowing what you are doing and why serves as the foundation of the Collins-Technique™ and achieving optimal performance. Good body awareness, core strength and stability is important for improving strength and decreasing stress loads on the body that can lead too muscle imbalance or injury. Core strength is also important for providing a stable base for the application of power through the limbs and enabling a smooth synergy between upper and lower body movement.

Implementing a training approach from the simple to more difficult exercises as well as quality of movement over quantity enables each participant to develop good body awareness and efficient movement patterns. From the onset, it is very important that you acquire attention to detail by focusing on the finer body adjustments required with each exercise. Some exercises within may appear easy or straightforward but each is essential in providing the building blocks and teaching points that carry over from one skill to the next. Variety and difficulty are added after the building blocks from each key movement pattern are mastered.

Using this specific body awareness approach allows your body to become more energy efficient in learning total body control. Over time it provides a greater outcome as less energy is being spent performing a similar movement. Creating a natural flowing body position using seemingly less effort is the trademark of a champion. A small percentage of athletes have progressed naturally to this point whilst others have to work smarter to achieve this goal, which serves as the foundation of the Collins-Technique™.

The Collins-Technique™ provides an exercise model that aims to help participants by:

- Providing an educational pathway for improving knowledge and understanding of core strength.
- Being more attentive to the finer details of core strength and stability exercises.
- Improving body awareness and posture in exercise by providing a framework of progressive core strength exercises and movement patterns.
- Improving gross motor patterns, coordination and breathing patterns.
- Improving muscular endurance of deep supporting postural muscles.
- Building a strong and efficient body with good strength endurance that has the ability to maintain better posture over longer periods of time.
- Improving neuromuscular firing patterns for better muscle synergy between the upper and lower body.
- Recognizing muscle imbalances and increasing strength in these areas to develop better body balance.
- Bringing muscle control and awareness of good posture throughout daily lifestyle activities.
- Choosing exercises appropriate to one's level of fitness.
- Applying the correct repetitions, sets and recovery periods.
- Introducing a core strength continuum to provide a benchmark of where the participant stands today and where to head to in the future.
- Promoting the importance of ongoing musculoskeletal and postural adjustments by a health professional (i.e. physiotherapist).
- Introducing an ongoing body maintenance routine of stretching, massage, relaxation and healthy eating for keeping the body in optimal working condition.

Core Stability

The muscles that provide core-stability are muscles that link the core-abdominal region, also known as the trunk or torso region, to the shoulder girdle and pelvic region, as shown below:

Section 1
Muscles that stabilize the torso – (spine and pelvis) including the rectus abdominis, obliques, quadratus lumborum, erector spinae and deeper transversus abdominis and multifidus muscles

Section 2
Muscles that maintain the position of the scapula including the trapezius, rhomboids, serratus anterior and rotator cuff muscles

Section 3
Muscles that stabilise the pelvis, leg and gluteal region and abdominal muscles

Exercising core muscles helps stabilize the torso, providing a strong and stable base that allows the effective transfer of forces throughout the body. A trim waistline from healthy eating and exercise and regular stretching also assists by improving one's center of gravity and good pelvic and spinal mobility.

Functional Joint Stability

Mechanically, the body can be considered as a series of segments that are connected at joints. The pliability and tension in muscles, tendons and ligaments affect the relative stability of joints. If these areas are weak, overstretched or hypermobile (an unusually large range of motion) the stability of a joint is reduced. Good nutrition is therefore extremely important in this process, especially in a child's growth and development. Subsequently, if any muscles undergo high levels of habitual mechanical stress, it can lead to muscle imbalances that also cause instability of joints by holding the joint in a less functional position. The ability of a joint to resist displacement and promote effective movement capabilities of the articulating body segments is one of the initial goals of the Collins-Technique™ that soon follows.

Introducing the appropriate exercises for each person requires thought to many factors including: motor coordination, movement mechanics, joint articulations, joint stability, mobility and range of motion, muscular strength, weakness or imbalance, and many others. The initial objective is to overcome traditional thinking of lifting heavy weights and instead applying a new approach focused on achieving core strength and stability using one's own body weight – just like a gymnast.

In order to successfully acquire muscle endurance that helps establish a strong foundation, the initial approach requires commitment to performing higher repetitions of lower intensity exercises with less recovery. Once essential joint stability and core strength endurance is enhanced, exercises are modified and progressed in difficulty and intensity with the adjustments of lever lengths and unstable surfaces such as using a fitness ball.

Hypermobility

Hypermobily refers to joints that can move far further than the average person's movement range due to increased joint and ligament laxity.

Some athletes are hypermobile throughout all their joints while others have specific joint hypermobility. What this means in real terms is that joints such as the ankles, knees and elbows, hyperextend beyond what is considered normal postural range. Swimmers are one example group with high levels of hyper-mobility of joints due to the non-weight bearing training environment they train in over many years. Thus, the importance of core strength training for swimmers to maintain joint stability. General hypermobility of joints is not normally a problem as long as adequate core strength is obtained.

Problems may arise when little is done and the gravitational forces take over at which point pain sets in. For instance, if a person who is hypermobile through the ankle, knee or hip region goes for a run, they are more likely to experience tenderness or pain in these areas due to the workload on supporting structures in terms of stability.

Developing the foot arch, improving leg alignment, squat mechanics and other drills as part of the Collins-Technique™ are prerequisites for improving functional joint stability. Not everyone with hypermobility will suffer pain or problems. As your Body Coach®, my goal is to simply advise you of the implications of what may occur if these elements are not taken into consideration as part of an overall training program. Undergoing a postural assessment by a qualified health professional such as a physiotherapist can help identify these imbalances and offer you a lifestyle solution.

Probably the most important element to consider for those with hypermobile joints is that some stretches that have become part of a warm-up routine may need to be replaced with stability drills. This is because stretching a hypermobile joint may overstretch ligaments supporting the joint causing a weakening effect rather than protective. Warm-up activities that bring attention to muscle control include isometric holds and bracing drills. In the meantime, ensure close contact with a health professional for specific joint stability exercises that suit your needs.

Hypermobility and Exercise

In order to achieve better joint stability, one must bring focus to the finer details of each exercise, by breaking the movement down into smaller segments. This enables better concentration on the task at hand and improved muscle control by ensuring good body posture and alignment. Attention to detail enables corrections and realignment to occur at regular intervals throughout the movement or exercise. When performing each exercise your goal is to continually monitor the body and make small postural corrections continually in order to keep the body aligned and build appropriate core strength and stability.

It is especially important for people with hypermobility to focus closely on correct tracking of the arms and legs in movement to avoid locking out the joints (hyperextension). This also helps keep muscles under tension ensuring core strength and stability is achieved. In some instances, you may have to reduce the range of motion of an exercise to ensure joint stability is developed. Attention to detail of the exercise and body position is of high priority – focusing on quality of movement over quantity.

The push-up exercise is one example of having to bring attention to detail when exercising. It is a great exercise for building core strength between the torso, hips and legs and torso, shoulders, chest and arms. If a participant is unable to maintain good form performing a push-up then the exercise intensity or exercise selection must be reduced and key movement patterns retrained. Good form with a push-up is shown in Figures 2, 4 and 6.

Starting with the arms kept close to the body when lowering and raising the body is vital in the development of core strength with push-up exercises. This involves good tracking of the arms, shoulder joint and shoulder blades. Caution must also be brought attention in controlling ones range of motion to ensure the arm muscles are held constantly under tension as opposed to being locked out. Because if you lower the body and then rise locking the arms out, as shown in Figure 1, stress generally

Fig 1: Poor Form

Avoid locking out elbows
(hyperextension)

Fig 2: Good Form

Maintain slightly bent arms and never
lock them out in order to maintain
muscles under tension

transfers across to the elbow joints, which needs to be avoided. The position of the arms therefore need to be held slightly bent in the starting and end positions for this to happen, as shown in Figure 2. This ensures muscles are under tension and can be strengthened and toned more effectively. Maintaining good alignment of the head and neck with the spine and pelvis is also vital in the development of good posture.

Body Alignment

Good body alignment from head to toe plays a vital role in achieving the best results in core strength training. Simply performing the movement without thought only builds bad postural habits that are often hard to correct. A sagging body position, as shown in Figure 3 can be a sign of poor body awareness, lack of joint strength and muscle control, which need to be corrected. A few simple adjustments of attention to detail, for instance – hip, abdominal, shoulders, hand, arm, elbow and head position – can help realign one's posture ensuring good body alignment, as shown in Figure 4.

THE BODY COACH

Fig 3: Poor Form

Arms locked, hips and shoulder region sagging

Fig 4: Good Form

Maintaining a strong core and good body and head alignment

Holding a static front support body position on one's hands and toes for short periods (i.e. 10–30 seconds) and then progressing to 30–60 seconds or more provides the pre-requisite isometric strength of the torso, lower back, shoulder, chest and arm region for progressing to the push-up exercise. Constant deep breathing keeps essential oxygenated blood reaching the muscles and allows carbon dioxide to be expelled from the body.

Time Under Tension

Maintaining muscle under tension whilst breathing deeply is an important element that is achieved by holding a static position for an extended period of time, such as the front support position held in Figure 4. In terms of a push-up progression, the static front support hold is a great transitional exercise in-between the kneeling push-up to normal push-ups on the toes. As one progresses from their knees to their toes (short to long lever), they may only be able to complete a few repetitions before loss of form. The key here is to continue the exercise by dropping back down onto your knees and

continuing until form is lost once more or muscle fatigue sets in. This builds muscle endurance and strong foundational strength that stays with you for a longer period of time.

To maintain time under tension of a muscle or series of muscles when exercising, certain exercises that are easy to perform can be increased in intensity by performing the exercise slower or creating an unstable environment that offers a challenge to the stabilizer and neutralizer muscles. This element plays a key role in determining repetitions (reps) and sets. For instance, if 10 push-ups can easily be performed in 10 seconds (1 second per rep), the intensity of the exercise can be increased by slowing the movement down to 2 or 3 seconds per rep. So, instead of 10 seconds the time under tension is now 20 or 30 seconds for the same amount of reps – making the exercise much harder to perform. Repetitions and sets are discussed in further depth in chapter 9.

Correct Movement Tracking

Position and correct movement tracking of the arms and legs in any exercise ensures optimal strength gains. Simply performing an exercise without focus puts tendons, ligaments and joints under excessive strain increasing the risk of injury. For instance, one's inability to maintain the arms against the body when lowering and raising the body in a close-grip push-up often translates to specific muscular weakness and poor arm and shoulder movement mechanics in various sporting endeavors, such as the arms swinging across the body when running or a short arm stroke in swimming.

The push-up exercise is once again used to demonstrate tracking of the arms. Compare the difference between the same exercise demonstrated in Figure 5 and Figure 6. Correct movement tracking; in this instance, keeping the arms close to the body (Figure 6) helps maintain good alignment of the arms and shoulder girdle, strengthening the muscles in the correct movement plane. Correct movement tracking of the arms and legs in exercise, daily movement and sporting activities improves posture, increases strength and reduces the risk of injury.

THE BODY COACH

Fig 5: Poor Form

Fig 6: Good Form

Elbows may be close when lowering body but splay out wide when rising due to muscular or joint weakness and poor body awareness

Abdominal muscles braced, elbows kept close to the body at all times when lowering and raising the body, with the head held in neutral position

Foot Arch Awareness

Flat feet are a common feature found in many people (Figure 7). Developing awareness of a natural arch (Figure 8) when on your feet helps establish muscle balance up the leg and through the hip region. Distributing one's weight across the footprint, towards the outside of the foot, to form an arch and healthy footprint is a great starting point in each standing exercise. It brings good body awareness for total body control and correct alignment from the feet through to the upper body.

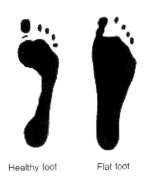

Healthy foot   Flat foot

Standing on a piece of newspaper and scrunching it up with your toes is one exercise that will help strengthen the foot arch. In exercise, distributing your weight to form a natural foot arch at the start of each exercise when standing creates synergy up the body by promoting the opportunity for more efficient movement patterns to occur.

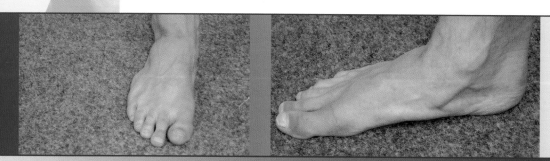

Fig. 7: Flat Feet – Rolled Inwards
Places stress on ankle, knee and hip regions when exercising and normal lifestyle activities. Note: See a podiatrist for orthotics (foot arch supports)

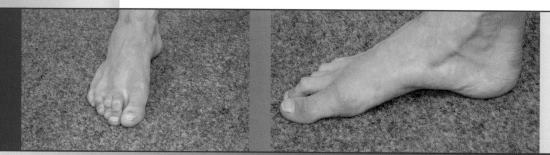

Fig. 8: Natural Arch
Helps maintain leg and hip alignment for improving movement mechanics and distributing the forces evenly

Good Leg Alignment

Flat feet can cause poor leg alignment, Figure 9, with the foot, ankle and knee rolling inwards and placing a large amount of undue stress on the large toes, ankle, knee and hip joints which can also lead to bunions. To help overcome this, realigning the leg starts at the feet. By rolling your weight towards the outside of the feet to form a healthy footprint (as shown in figure 8), the ankle and knee can realign themselves with the weight now positioned over the center of the foot as shown in Figure 10. Simultaneously rolling the feet and knees out helps realign the leg and distribute one's body weight evenly. This simple movement can have a major impact on overall leg and body alignment as shown on the opposite page:

THE BODY COACH

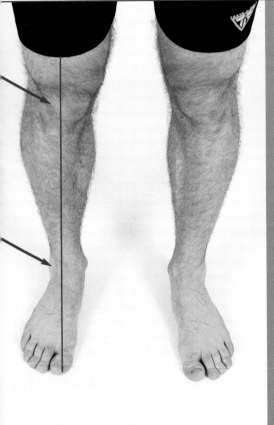

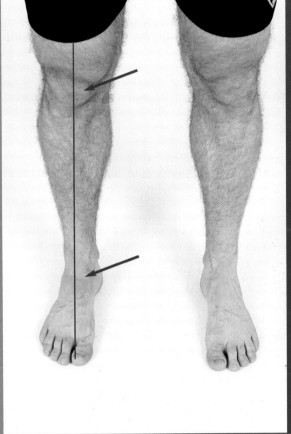

Fig. 9: Poor Leg Alignement
Flat feet can lead to the knees
rolling inwards and stress on the
large toe, knee and hip regions. In
some instances causing bunions
or shin, knee and hip pain when
standing, walking or running.

Fig. 10: Good Leg Alignement
Establishing a healthy foot arch
improves ankle, knee, hip and
overall leg alignment

Chapter 2

Key Elements – 3B's Principle™

Every core strength exercise has a number of key elements to consider when setting up and performing a movement. Applying correct technique from the onset will help strengthen the body and the mind. Building core strength relies on correct recruitment of the appropriate muscles at all times. The key elements required in order to maintain good body position whilst exercising fall under a classification I've termed the 3B's Principle™:

- Brace
- Breath
- Body Position

1. Brace

(1a) Neutral Spine

The term 'neutral spine' refers to the natural alignment of the spine. To help improve the health of our spine, it is important to develop better awareness of our body position by practicing the 'neutral spine' position – sitting, kneeling, lying (front and back), standing and moving. Regular practice in these positions helps develop a sense of control into our muscle memory, so in time we adjust these positions naturally.

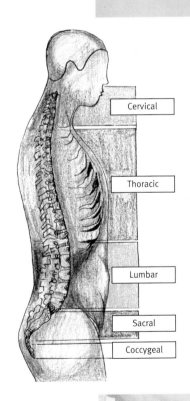

The main curves of the spine are:
- **Cervical spine (C1-C7):** the rear of the neck curves slightly inwards
- **Thoracic spine (T1-T12):** the upper to mid area of the back curves slightly outwards
- **Lumbar spine (L1-L5):** the lower back curves slightly inwards
- **Sacral spine (S1-S5):** the bottom of your spine curves slightly outwards and links to the coccygeal

A good starting point in finding neutral spine position is by lying on your back with your knees bent (Figure 11). As you begin to move your spine and pelvis gently through a range of motion by flattening the lower back to the ground then arching upwards – the goal is to find a mid-point between the two that makes you feel comfortable. This is called neutral spine position. A similar movement of the pelvic region is used when sitting and standing.

Fig. 11

(1b) Abdominal Bracing

Abdominal bracing is important because it teaches you to contract your stomach muscles, increasing awareness of your body position as well as helping protect your lower back region. The combination of neutral spine position, bracing and breathing is essential to adapt and master, as it will enhance movement mechanics. Abdominal Bracing in association with neutral spine position holds an important role in maintaining good posture and can be performed sitting, lying, kneeling, standing or walking throughout the day.

The abdominal bracing and breathing combinations will be referred to throughout this book as a reference point as most exercises – for example, "find neutral spine position, brace abdominal muscles and breathe deeply." Practiced regularly you will naturally learn to adapt to these positions.

Abdominal Bracing 4-Point Kneeling example:

INSTRUCTION

Fig. 12: Stomach Muscles Relaxed

Fig. 13: Stomach Muscle Braced and Neutral Spine Maintained

In the 4-point kneeling position, on your hands and knees, draw your belly (navel) button inwards towards your spine and hold without changing your neutral spine position. Using deep breaths, continue breathing in through your nose and out your mouth whilst holding this inwards braced position of the stomach for five breaths or more. Relax and repeat. Initially, breathing may feel short and the stomach hard to hold in, but with practice you will improve your ability to brace and breathe more efficiently, without tensing other muscles of the body.

Research suggests that the deep muscles are best exercised at low intensity, and suggest that levels of 30-40% of maximal voluntary contraction (MVC) are most favorable. The idea is to pull the stomach in from the navel region and activate the pelvic floor muscles to learn how to control the deeper

muscles to release and hold at this level. The reason for this is that the stabilizing muscles are postural muscles that work continuously at low levels of maximal muscle contraction throughout the day. Hence, to increase the intensity of the 4-point kneeling exercise you can:

- Increase the time you hold this position by the number of deep breaths you perform and number of sets.
- Introduce movement of the arms and limbs into the equation.
- Increase the lever length from the knees up onto the toes into a front support position.
- Add movement into the equation whilst bracing the abdominal muscles, such as moving into the push-up exercise.

2. Breathing

Throughout normal everyday activities, the nervous system usually controls respirations automatically to meet the body's demands without our conscious concern. When we are passive, or at rest our demands for oxygen are small and breathing is slow and shallow. When there is an increased demand for oxygen, breathing becomes much deeper and swifter. When you start to exercise or move more rapidly, carbon dioxide from the muscle is pushed into the blood. This triggers a signal in the brain to make you breathe faster and deeper so that you supply more oxygenated blood to your working muscles.

One of the main functions of your respiratory system is to get oxygen from the air outside into the blood, and then expel carbon dioxide waste from the blood out into the atmosphere. Although the basic rhythm of respiration is set and coordinated by the respiratory center (neurologically), the rhythm can be modified in response to the demands of the body. In other words, breathing can be controlled voluntarily to some extent through conscious concern.

Fig. 14: Breathe tall and deep into the lungs through the nose

Fig. 15: Breathe out through pursed lips

To maximize training results, draw in air deeply through the nose (Figure 14) and breathe out (Figure 15) in a slow controlled manner through the mouth through pursed lips (like blowing out candles) for a count of three. Deep breathing is practiced whilst maintaining neutral spine position, abdominal bracing and exercising.

This type of breathing results in the lungs being able to take in more air in a controlled manner. As more oxygen is taken into the bloodstream, the muscle's waste product carbon dioxide is expelled more efficiently, especially as you become fitter.

The breathing focus when performing the Core Strength Exercises is to control the rhythm of one's oxygen supply by being conscious of one's breathing patterns. This requires an approach of breathing tall like a ballet dancer or standing as a prince or princess does whilst maintaining neutral spine and strong abdominal brace position.

In core strength training, breathing generally flows in the following way:

- Breathe out when you exert a force (e.g. rise up in push-up exercise)
- Breathe in with recovery (e.g. lowering down in push-up exercise)

3. Body Position

One's ability to hold a good body position – *neutral spine, effective abdominal brace and breathing pattern* – whilst working the extremities, is crucial in terms of reducing stress on the lower back and maximizing core strength. By adapting the 3B's Principle™ outlined, you will build a unique internal understanding of your body, its muscles and how they respond to various movements. Adapting the posture of a ballet dancer (for example) in terms of body position is one way to ensure good body position is maintained whilst exercising.

As core strength improves the lever length can be increased. In exercise, a lever is the length and angle of a muscle or pair of muscles from a joint. Increasing the joint angle generally increases the intensity of the exercise, especially when working against gravity. Yet, if we shorten the lever or decrease the joint angle, we generally reduce the intensity by distributing the load. Whichever the case, good body position must be maintained.

The push-up exercise is a prime example. A Kneeling Push-up (Figure 16) shortens the lever length and the demand placed on the lower back, where as a normal push-up (Figure 17) performed on the toes increases the lever length and the load placed on the lower back. This is why learning neutral spine position and abdominal bracing is so important in the beginning. Contraction of the stomach muscles in neutral spine helps reduce the load on the lower back region, to stop it from arching or sagging.

As one progresses through the exercises and principles as outlined, they will begin to develop a unique understanding of their body, its movement and muscle control. In all exercises, ensure good head, neck, spine and pelvic alignment is maintained at all times with the rest of the body for the development of good posture. The overall focus of each exercise should therefore be on quality of the movement by maintaining a good body position.

THE BODY COACH

Fig. 16: Short Lever
Low load

Fig. 17: Long Lever
High load

Maintaining Good Body Position through Self-Spotting

To assist in maintaining good body alignment, a self-spotting approach can be used as a way to ensure good body position whilst performing exercises that may often be beyond one's capability and overlooked – such as a chin-up. For some people, performing body weight exercises such as chin-ups or chest dips are often replaced with alternative exercises or simply avoided due to one's inability to lift their own body weight. The first approach in the core strength continuum is performing the appropriate exercise that builds the essential endurance of the muscle whilst maintaining a good body position. The second approach involves 'self-spotting,' which is a way of reducing the body load through the assistance of the arms or legs.

For example: placing a bench under one foot when performing the chin-up or chest dip exercise allows the participant to decrease the load of the exercise on the targeted upper body region. The idea is to allow the participant to perform the

Fig. 18: STARTING POSITION
In chin-up position with arms
gripping overhead bar, place one
foot up on a bench

Fig. 19: MIDPOINT
Use leg to assist chin-up
movement and to maintain a good
body position

movement using both the arms and the leg and become confident in doing so. Over time, the participant can vary how much assistance comes from the legs in terms of effort. One example is performing as many chin-ups as possible using your own bodyweight, before adding the self-spotting technique (foot on bench) to help complete each repetition and set. Using this approach will help each participant gain strength and confidence and maintaining correct muscular tracking in a relatively short period of time, building a good core strength base. Figures 18 and 19 shows one example of the self-spotting approach used when performing a chin-up.

As the participant becomes stronger, the assistance of the leg is reduced or eliminated with the back and arm muscles doing the work.

THE BODY COACH

Chapter 3

Isometric Strength Exercises

Fig. 20: POOR FORM
- Sagging between the shoulder blades
- Weak head and neck position
- Poor abdominal contraction and lower back position causing sagging

Fig. 21: GOOD FORM
- The shoulders are raised
- Pelvis and abdominal muscles realigned in neutral position
- Strong abdominal brace
- The head and neck are aligned in neutral position

Isometric exercises are used to improve the neuromuscular link throughout the body. Being able to hold a static body position effectively whilst exercising improves postural awareness, strength and muscle control. With the assistance of the 3B's Principle™ each participant will learn how to monitor and readjust to the appropriate body position maximizing the time muscle is held under tension. In most exercises the challenge is placed upon muscles and their associated joints. The challenge comes from being able to hold the core region and joints in their neutral position whilst fatigue sets in throughout the body. In the front support exercise, the base of support for the body is the hands and feet. In order to keep the body and head aligned in its more efficient neutral position the 3B's Principle™ is applied.

Identifying poor form in this position (Figure 20) and making the appropriate body adjustments with the assistance of a coach to find the correct body position (Figure 21) makes all the difference in building your best body ever. Maintaining focus on the finer details of controlling one's body position is the key priority. In this instance, the progression comes from being able to perform a push-up whilst holding an isometric body position. The following exercises focus on isometric strengthening of the body.

Exercise 1 – Front Support Holds (1a-1e)

Target Area(s): Chest, shoulders and arm muscles; abdominal muscles and pelvic alignment; head and neck alignment

1a. Level 1 – LOW INTENSITY

1b. Level 2 – MEDIUM INTENSITY

1c. Level 3 – HIGH INTENSITY
Raise one leg whilst maintaining a streamline body position

1d. Level 4 (unstable surface)
HIGH INTENSITY
1e: Increase the intensity by raising one leg off ball

INSTRUCTION
- Kneel on ground and place hands in front of the body shoulder-width apart.
- Rise up onto toes and lean shoulders and body forward to ensure eye line is forward of fingers.
- Brace abdominal muscles and ensure neutral spine position is held.
- Hold strong body position as you continue to breathe deeply in and out for set period of time (i.e. 10-60 seconds or more).

NOTE
- Regular small body readjustments are required to maintain good body alignment in all exercises.
- The challenge is progressed through Exercises 2-7 below then onto push-up exercises involving movement of the arms or joint angle.

Exercise 2 – Arm Angle Front Support

Extension to the challenge of the core is achieved by increasing the lever length – varying the angle of the arms and holding this position. The position of the core is held in a banana shape throughout from the feet to the shoulder region.

Target Area(s): Chest, shoulders and arm muscles; head and neck alignment, abdominal muscles (isometrically) and pelvis alignment.

2a. SHORT LEVER – ON KNEES

POSITION 1 – FRONT SUPPORT
POSITION 2 – EXTEND ARMS
POSITION 3 – ARMS EXTEND OUTWARDS (Advanced level only)
- Limit arm range to suit current strength ability.
- Beginners only perform Positions 1 and 2.
- More advanced athletes can advance to Position 3.

INSTRUCTION
- Start in a four-point kneeling position on hands and knees.
- Lean shoulders and body forward to ensure eye line is forward of fingers.
- Brace abdominal muscles and ensure neutral spine position.
- Hold front support position for 5 seconds then move hands forward 10 cm and repeat.
- Maintain these small incremental movements of the hand and holding times until you lose form (i.e. lower back sags) or fatigue sets in with lower back or arms. If so, stop the exercise, rest and recover.

NOTE
- Limit arm range extended to suit current strength ability. Beginners only perform Positions 1 and 2. More advanced athletes can advance to Position 3.

THE BODY COACH

2b. LONG LEVER – ON TOES
(Advanced only exercise)

POSITION 1 – FRONT SUPPORT

POSITION 2 – ARMS EXTEND

POSITION 3 – ARMS EXTEND OUTWARDS (Advanced level only)
- The position of the core is held in a banana shape position
- Ensure neutral head and neck alignment is maintained.
- Limit arm range to suit current strength ability.

INSTRUCTION
- Start in a Front Support position on hands with toes pointed.
- Hold front support position for five seconds then move hands forward 10 cm or so and hold for another five seconds.
- Maintain these small incremental movements of the hand and holding times until you lose form (lower back sags) or fatigue (arms fatigue), then stop, rest and recover.

NOTE
- Limit arm range extended to suit current strength ability through shoulders and abdominal region.
- Master Exercise 2a on your knees first before attempting 2b.
- Ensure head and neck alignment is maintained at all times with the rest of the body for the development of good posture.

Exercise 3 – Front Support Fitness Ball Holds: Elbows

Target Area(s): Shoulders, arms, abdominal muscles, pelvis.

**3a. LEVEL 1
FOREARMS AND KNEES**

**3B. LEVEL 1
FOREARMS AND TOES**

INSTRUCTION
- Start in a Front Support position, resting on elbows and forearms with clenched fists; 3a – Knees on ground. 3b – Toes on ground
- Lean the body forward until eye line is over clenched fists. This ensures strong shoulder position and braced abdominal muscles.
- Hold Front Support position breathing deeply in and out for set period of time without losing abdominal brace or loss of body position.

NOTE
- Maintain strong abdominal brace.
- To increase the challenge, one leg can be raised and held a few inches whilst maintaining a strong core.
- Do not allow hips to tilt or any stress or pain to radiate to the lower back region. Always stop the exercise if this occurs.
- For stability purposes, lean the fitness ball against the wall when first starting out.

THE BODY COACH

Exercise 4 – (a) Prone Elbow Support (b) Prone Elbow to Front Support

Target Area(s): Chest, shoulders, arms, abdominal muscles.

4a. Prone elbow support

INSTRUCTION 4a. Prone elbow support
- Start in a Front Support position, resting on elbows and forearms with clenched fists on the ground.
- Lean the body forward until eye line is over clenched fists. This ensures strong shoulder position and braced abdominal muscles.
- Maintaining strong abdominal brace – keeping back flat – whilst breathing in and out deeply for 5-10 breaths or more without losing form.
- Focus on bracing the abdominals for length of drill.

4b.
1. START
2. Raise onto one hand

3. RAISE ONTO BOTH HANDS
4. LOWER ONTO ONE FOREARM AND THEN BACK TO START POSITION (1)

5. LOWER ONTO BOTH FOREARMS

INSTRUCTION 4b. Prone elbow to front support

- Start in a Front Support position, resting on elbows and forearms with clenched fists on the ground.
- Lean the body forward until eye line is over clenched fists. This ensures strong shoulder position and braced abdominal muscles.
- Start by raising up form one forearm onto hand.
- Maintaining strong abdominal brace rise up onto other hand into a Front Support raised position – hands and toes.
- Reverse sequence and lower back to forearms.

NOTE

- Perform movement continuously up and down without twisting, tilting or waddling of the hips for set amount of reps or loss of form.
- Maintain strong shoulder and abdominal positions throughout exercise.

THE BODY COACH

Exercise 5 – Fitness Ball Walk-Out

Target Area(s): Chest, shoulders, arms, abdominal muscles, pelvis and legs.
Equipment: Fitness Ball

1. LIE ON BALL
2. MIDPOINT (Beginner / Intermediate level)
3. MIDPOINT (Inter/Advanced level)
4. MIDPOINT (Advanced level) ON TOES
5. On toes
6. Leg raised

INSTRUCTION
- Lie on ball on stomach with hands and feet on the ground.
- Slowly roll forward onto hands and brace abdominal muscles.
- Maintain deep breathing pattern whilst walking hands forward.
- Keep abdominal muscles tight and lifted as the ball reaches the legs and works towards the feet. Resist any arching or sagging of the lower back.
- Hold briefly and return to starting position maintaining control of your body and the ball until you rest at the starting position.

NOTE
- Beginners start by walking out to midpoint (2) only.
- As strength improves, progress with good form to position (3) avoiding any lower back sagging.
- Ensure head and neck alignment is maintained at all times with the rest of the body for the development of good posture before progressing to 4, 5 and 6 on toes with one leg raised.

Exercise 6 – Isometric Rear Supports

Target Area(s): Chest, shoulders, arms, abdominal muscles, lower back, pelvis and legs.

Starting Position   **Raised Midpoint**

INSTRUCTION
- Sit on ground with hands behind body and legs extended, feet together.
- Raise hips up and hold extended position with strong abdominal brace and deep breathing pattern until loss of form, whether 3 or 30 seconds, then lower and stretch.

NOTE
- Always perform this exercise under the guidance of a trainer.
- Ensure body alignment and deep breathing pattern is maintained throughout holding pattern.

Exercise 7 – Fitness Ball Isometric Rear Supports

Target Area(s): Chest, shoulders, arms, abdominal muscles, lower back, pelvis and legs.

Equipment: Fitness Ball

Level 1
- Lie on back, flex at hip and rest feet on ball.
- Extend arms on floor at 45 degree angle to body.
- Breathing out slowly raise buttocks, hips and back off ground. Hold extended body position breathing deeply.
- Breathe in and lower.

Level 2
- Lie on back, flex at hip and rest feet on ball.
- Bend elbows and rest across triceps with fingers pointed towards sky.
- Breathing out slowly raise buttocks, hips and back off ground. Hold extended body position breathing deeply.
- Breathe in and lower.

Level 3
- Lie on back, flex at hip and rest feet on ball.
- Cross arms across chest.
- Breathing out slowly raise buttocks, hips and back off ground. Hold extended body position breathing deeply.
- Breathe in and lower.

NOTE
- Have a trainer assist all holding patterns with one hand supporting the lower back and the other behind the knee or the ball.
- Ensure the participant is breathing deeply and not holding breath.

LEVEL 1 – Arms Flat

LEVEL 1 – Body Raised

Level 2 – Elbows Bent

LEVEL 2 – Body Raised

LEVEL 3 – Arms across Chest

Level 3 – Body Raised

THE BODY COACH

Exercise 8 – Body Dish

Target Area(s): Abdominal muscles, pelvis and hip flexors (iliopsoas).

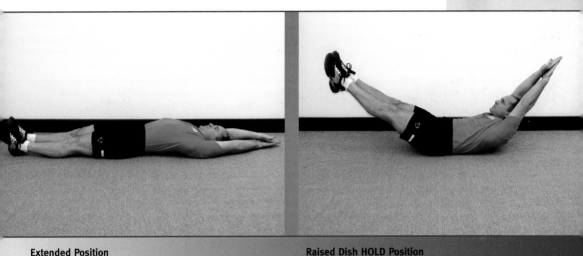

Extended Position
Raised Dish HOLD Position

INSTRUCTION
* Lie in an extended position – legs together, toes pointed; arms overhead, hands together.

8a – Repetitions: Bracing your core abdominal region contract musculature and simultaneously raise arms and legs into a body dish (banana) position, then lower without relaxing. Breathe out as you rise up (dish) and breathe in as you lower. Maintain long streamlined position whilst performing 8 or more repetitions.

8b – Dish Holds: Rise into dish position and hold, ensuring deep breathing and strong abdominal brace is maintained for a set period of time (i.e. 5 seconds or longer).

Exercise 9 – Body Dish Rolls

1. Start
2. Roll to side
3. Roll onto back

4. Across to opposite side
5. Returning to starting position

INSTRUCTION

- **Body Rolls:** Rise into dish position, then slowly roll onto side, then stomach maintaining a long extended body position. As you roll the body, the legs and arms need to adjust accordingly when rolling onto side then stomach before returning to the first dish position on your back. Ensure muscle synergy, speed of movement and body position is maintained. Perform single or multiple rolls across a clear floor going left and right ways. Maintaining a straight line is the athlete's goal.

Exercise Tips:

- Use carpeted floor or exercise mats and ensure a clear open space when performing body roll.
- Maintain total muscle control and contraction until drill is completed.
- Start with 180-degree rolls left and right sides, before progressing to more advanced 360-degree and 720-degree and beyond rolls.

THE BODY COACH

ISOMETRIC STRENGTHENING EXERCISES

1a. Front Support Holds

Hold for__secs,__times

1b. Front Support - Point Toes

Hold for__secs,__times

**1c. Front Support
– Raise One Leg (Left and Right)**

Hold for__secs,__times

1d. Front Support Hold on Fitness Ball

Hold for__secs,__times

2a. Arm Angle Front Support - Knees

Hold for__secs,__times

2b. Arm Angle Front Support - Toes

Hold for__secs,__times

3a. Front Support Fitness Ball Holds (Elbows)

3b. Front Support Fitness ball Holds (Toes)

Hold for__secs,__times

Hold for__secs,__times

4a. Prone Elbow Support

4b. Prone Elbow to Front Support

Hold for__secs,__times

Hold for__secs,__times

5. Fitness Ball Walk-out

6. Isometric Rear Supports

Hold for__secs,__times

Hold for__secs,__times

THE BODY COACH

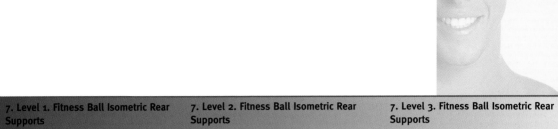

7. Level 1. Fitness Ball Isometric Rear Supports

Hold for__secs,__times

7. Level 2. Fitness Ball Isometric Rear Supports

Hold for__secs,__times

7. Level 3. Fitness Ball Isometric Rear Supports

Hold for__secs,__times

8. Body Dish

Hold for__secs,__times

7c. Body Roll Sequence

Perform__sets,__reps

Chin-up isometric hold See midpoint (Ex. 78)

Hold for__secs,__times

Chapter 4

Abdominals and Lower Back

Strength of the abdominal mechanism is important because it controls not only the position of the pelvis but also the relationship of the shoulder girdle and thorax, abdominal cavity and pelvic region. Abdominal wall musculature without adequate endurance, strength and coordination is more likely to permit surrounding tissues to be taken past their physiological limit.

To ensure good effective abdominal strength gains one must also take into consideration their daily eating plan for maintaining a trim waistline, lower body fat levels as well as keeping muscles of the hip and surrounding areas free of muscular tension to ensure good pelvic mobility.

As part of the Core strength Continuum summarized in Chapter 9, exercises are often progressed through a series of core-isometric bracing and breathing drills to build static postural endurance. This is then followed by exercises involving a range of movement for the abdominal region as follows:

Exercise 10 – Abdominal Bracing: Supine Position

Target Area(s): Lower abdominals and respiratory (bracing and deep breathing).

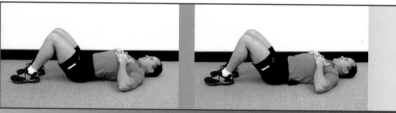

Relaxed | Braced

INSTRUCTION

- Lie on your back with knees bent and place the LumbAtube™ or a half-rolled towel under the largest arch of lower back. As you become stronger, remove these items.
- Breathing in through the nose, then out through the mouth with pursed lips draw your navel (belly button) inwards and hold whilst continuing breathing.
- Focus on relaxing the rest of the body whilst maintaining a strong abdominal brace.
- Your aim is to focus on the inwards contraction of the stomach without releasing for a set time frame or controlled number of breaths.
- Initially breathing may be short, but over time will become deeper as the diaphragm muscles strengthen and coordination improves. Deep breathing is important in every exercise helping improve body awareness, lung capacity and oxygen exchange.

Special Note: This exercise forms the foundation for obtaining a strong core. Most exercises within this book require Abdominal Bracing when performing the exercise. Maintaining a strong brace and deep breathing pattern ensures good form is maintained. The ability to hold the brace from start to finish is the participant's goal in each exercise.

Exercise 11 – Abdominal Bracing: Supine Position (Leg and Arms Challenge)

The next challenge to the abdominal brace comes from introducing exercises that involve movement of the arms or legs or both together. Learning to hold the abdominal brace whilst performing arm or leg movement in a variety of positions helps improve motor coordination. Ultimately, abdominal bracing helps maintain exercise technique and the ability to build endurance, which is required before speed or power movements of the arms, or legs are introduced. Abdominal bracing in line with neutral spine position and deep breathing forms the foundation of all exercises within this book.

INSTRUCTION
- Lie on your back with knees bent and place the LumbAtube™ or a half-rolled towel under the largest arch of lower back. As you become stronger, remove these items.
- Breathing in through the nose, then out through the mouth with pursed lips draw your navel (belly button) inwards and hold whilst continuing breathing.
- Focus on relaxing the rest of the body whilst maintaining a strong abdominal brace.
- Your aim is to focus on the inwards contraction of the stomach without releasing for a set time frame or controlled number of breaths whilst moving the leg in the following manner:
  Level 1: bent leg raised
  Level 2: leg slide
  Level 3: straight leg raised
- Slowly move one leg through activity for 5-10 breaths, then repeat with opposite leg.
- Initially breathing may be short, but over time will become deeper as the diaphragm muscles strengthen and coordination improves. Deep breathing is important in every exercise helping improve body awareness, lung capacity and oxygen exchange.

11a. Level 1 – Starting position

Level 1 – Bent leg raised

11b. Level 2 – Leg bent

Level 2 – Leg slide

11c. Level 3 – Leg straight

Level 3 – Straight Leg raised

THE BODY COACH

Exercise 12 – Abdominal Bracing: Prone Position

Relaxed   Braced

INSTRUCTION
- Lie on your stomach with hands placed under your chin.
- Breathing in through the nose, then out through the mouth with pursed lips draw your belly button inwards and hold – bracing the abdominal muscles and continuing to breathe deeply.
- Hold body position for 5-10 breaths.

Exercise Tips:
- Focus on relaxing the rest of the body, especially the buttocks muscles when bracing the abdominal muscles upwards off the ground.
- Your aim is to focus on the inwards contraction of the stomach without releasing for a set time frame or controlled number of breaths.
- Initially breathing may be short, but over time the association between your diaphragm, lungs and abdominal brace will improve with regular participation, making the exercise become easier for the same amount of effort.

Exercise 13 – Abdominal Slide

START	MIDPOINT
Hands on Thighs	Hands slide up to Knees

INSTRUCTION

- Lie on your back with knees bent and place the LumbAtube™ or a half-rolled towel under the largest arch of lower back and rest hands on thighs.
- Breathing in through the nose, then out through the mouth with pursed lips draw your navel (belly button) inwards and hold – bracing the abdominal muscles.
- Maintaining a strong abdominal brace, forcefully breathe out through pursed lips, whilst sliding hands up thighs for a count of three until palms reach the knees.
- Breathe in as you lower for a count of "three."

Exercise Tips:

- Maintain a neutral head and neck position with the body throughout the exercise.
- Avoid stooping the head forward when rising up – this is a sign of poor body awareness and weak neck and abdominal muscles.
- As strength improves, remove LumbAtube™ and/or half-rolled towel and complete exercises without assistance.

THE BODY COACH

Exercise 14 – Abdominal Crunch Series

14a. Level 1. ARMS FOLDED ACROSS CHEST

Level 1 - MIDPOINT
Hands slide up to knees

14b. Level 2. HANDS BEHIND HEAD

Level 2 - Increase resistance by increasing the lever length with hands touching back of head

14c. Level 3. ARMS EXTENDED OVERHEAD

Level 3 - Maintain extended arm position overhead in a streamline position when raising

INSTRUCTION
- Lie on your back with knees bent with the LumbAtube™ or a half-rolled towel under the largest arch of lower back and rest hands on thighs.
- 14a. Level 1. Fold hands across chest (short lever)
- 14b. Level 2. place hands behind head (mid lever)
- 14c. Level 3. extend arms overhead (long Lever)
- Maintaining a strong abdominal brace, forcefully breathe out through pursed lips, whilst raising shoulders off ground and crunching stomach (ribs to pelvis).
- Breathe in as you lower.

Exercise Tips:
- Maintain a neutral head and neck position with the body throughout the exercise.
- Avoid stooping the head forward when rising up – this is a sign of poor body awareness and weak neck and abdominal muscles.
- As strength improves, remove LumbAtube™ and/or half-rolled towel and complete exercises without assistance.
  Note: The extension of the 'lever length' increases the intensity of the abdominal contraction.

Exercise 15 – Medicine Ball Coordination Crunch

START
Knees bent and arms extended

MIDPOINT
Raise arms and one Leg

INSTRUCTION
- Lie on your back with legs bent and arms extended overhead holding Medicine Ball.
- Bracing the abdominal muscles as you breathe out, simultaneously raise the arms, shoulders and one leg to crunch, and then lower.
- Repeat lifting opposite leg.

Exercise Tips:
- Aim for good timing between upper and lower body.
- Keep exercise slow and under control for optimal strength gains.

THE BODY COACH

Exercise 16 – Fitness Ball: Abdominal Crunch Sequence (a–d)

16a. Level 1
Arms extended forward

Level 1 - MIDPOINT – Curl-up

16b. Level 2 – Hands across chest

Level 2 - MIDPOINT – Curl-up

16c. Level 3 – Hands behind head

Level 3 - MIDPOINT – Curl-up

INSTRUCTION

- Lie on ball on arch of back, legs bent and feet shoulder-width apart.
- Level 1: Arms extended forward
- Level 2: Hands across chest
- Level 3: Hands behind head
- Level 4: Arms extended overhead
- Level 5: Arms extended overhead holding medicine ball
- Contracting the abdominal muscles and breathing out, slowly crunch and curl the stomach muscles up (similar to a banana shape), without moving the hips or rolling on the ball, then lower – breathing in.
- Perform the exercise slow to feel a slight burning sensation from the contraction of the stomach muscles.
- Maintain the head in its neutral position throughout to avoid neck tension.
- Ensure the ball remains still whilst raising and lowering.

16d. Level 4 – Arms extended

Level 4 - MIDPOINT – Curl-up

16e. Level 5 – Arms extended holding medicine ball

Level 5 - MIDPOINT – Curl-up holding ball

Exercise Tips:

- Aim for good timing between upper and lower body.
- Keep exercise slow and under control for optimal strength gains.
- Maintain regular breathing pattern.
- Ensure correct technique at all times to ensure abdominal muscles are being worked.

Note: Level 1 progresses from short lever to long lever. In other words, low to higher intensity effort.

Exercise 17 – The Hundred Drill

RAISE LEGS AND ARMS

PULSE ARMS UP AND DOWN

INSTRUCTION
- Lie on your back knees bent arms by your side.
- Breathing out, curl upper body and raise legs to approximately 110 degree leg angle and arms parallel to ground, palms facing downwards.
- Holding this position with a strong abdominal brace and shoulders raised off the ground and head and neck held neutral, pulse the arms up and down through a 30 cm range.
- Breathe out applying a pulse motion as the arms raise up and down.
- Pulse arms 20 times then rest with a total of 5 sets to reach 100 pulses – The Hundred Drill.
- Work towards completing one hundred pulses in one set over time.

Exercise Tips:
- Legs can be bent with feet flat on the ground if abdominal weakness is present (Beginner level).
- Legs may also be bent at 90 degrees at the hip and knee in the air (Intermediate level).

Exercise 18 – Medicine Ball Raise

START   MIDPOINT

INSTRUCTION
- Lie on your back with legs raised from hip at 90 degrees and slightly bent.
- Extend arms up above eye line holding Medicine Ball.
- Breathing out, raise shoulders off the ground and reach Medicine Ball up towards feet, then lower.

Exercise Tips:
- Avoid swinging legs or taking hip angle beyond 90 degrees due to the stress placed on the lower back region.
- Keep head neutral at all times. Avoid leading with chin, use abdominal muscles and maintain good form.

THE BODY COACH

OBLIQUES

Exercise 19 – Lateral Side Raises

START   MIDPOINT – LEGS AND ARMS RAISED

INSTRUCTION

- Lie on your side, legs extended, toes pointed and feet together.
- The arm closest to the ground extends above head with palm facing towards ceiling – head relaxed resting on inner part of arm.
- The upper arm is bent, supporting your body weight in front of the body.
- Draw your navel inwards and hold – maintaining a neutral spine.
- Maintaining a long body position, forcefully breathe out through pursed lips and simultaneously raise legs and arm into the air, then lower.
- Repeat on opposite side for set amount of repetitions or time.

Exercise Tips:

- Maintain tight and long body position by leaning body slightly forward and putting weight onto hand supporting the body. Avoid leaning or falling backwards.
- Increase speed of movement for continuous up and down movement.

Exercise 20 – Abdominal Oblique: Chest Crossover Sequence

INSTRUCTION
Lie on your back in the following positions:

- **20a. Level 1:** Knees bent, arms folded across chest. Lift head and shoulders from the floor while angling body across to one side. Complete set and repeat across to the opposite side.
- **20b. Level 2:** Knees bent, hands behind head. Rise across towards one knee, lower, then rise across to the other side.
- **20c. Level 3:** Knee bent, one foot resting on the opposite knee. Raise opposite elbow to opposite knee. Repeat opposite side.
- **20d. Level 4:** On one side bend knee and place hand behind head. On the other side, straighten leg and raise into air and place arm on ground. Bending straight leg, meet elbow of opposite arm, then extend out again.
- **20e. Level 5:** Knee bent, one foot resting on the opposite knee with Medicine Ball resting on shoulder. Raise opposite elbow to opposite knee.
- **20f. Level 6 (advanced only):** On one side bend knee and raise into air and place hand behind head. On the other side, straighten leg and raise into air and place arm on ground. Bending straight leg, meet elbow of opposite arm, then extend out again. Ensure strong abdominal brace is maintained at all times to protect lower back.

Exercise Tips:
- Repeat all exercises on opposite side.
- These exercises progress from simple (Level 1) to more advanced exercises of a higher intensity (Level 6). Ensure good posture is maintained at all times.
- Never exercise with any pain. Stop exercise if form lapses.
- Maintain deep controlled breathing pattern.

THE BODY COACH

20a. LEVEL 1: ARMS ACROSS CHEST

Crossover

20b. LEVEL 2: ARMS behind head

Crossover

20c. LEVEL 3: Knee bent, one arm behind head

Elbow to knee

20d. Level 4

Elbow to knee

20e. LEVEL 5

Elbow to knee with medicine ball

20f. Level 6 – both legs raised (advanced)

Elbow to knee

Exercise 21 – Medicine Ball Twist

START

MIDPOINT

INSTRUCTION
- Sit back at 45–60 degree angle and brace abdominal muscles. Avoid rounding the back.
- Extend arms forward holding Medicine Ball.
- Maintaining a strong abdominal brace, slowly take the Medicine Ball across to the left knee then back across to the right knee.
- This exercise places a demand on the isometric abdominal brace being held by working the medicine ball at different angles.

Exercise Tips:
- Keep the abdominal muscles braced and pelvis square.
- Keep movements short, moving arms from knee-to-knee without twisting the lower back.
- Avoid going beyond the outside of the knees with a ball.

THE BODY COACH

Exercise 22 – Fitness Ball Oblique Twists

Level 1 – Hands only START

Twist onto shoulder

Level 2: Add weighted medicine ball

Twist onto shoulder

INSTRUCTION
- Level 1: Lie on ball at shoulder height across shoulder blades. Feet shoulder-width apart, arms extended above chest, hands together.
- Raise hip and body parallel to ground.
- Contract the abdominal region and breathe out as you slowly lower the arms to the left side - simultaneously rotating the hip, torso and shoulders across the ball until arms are parallel to ground.
- Allow rotation of the hips and bending of the knee to limit stress on lower back. To complete the movement you will roll across onto shoulder on ball and breathe in.
- Keeping arms extended, repeat movement by rotating across the ball to the right side.

PROGRESSION
- Level 2: To increase the intensity of the exercise and oblique activation, add a weight or resistance such as a Medicine Ball to the movement.

Exercise Tips:
- Maintain head in neutral position throughout.
- Maintain deep breathing pattern.

Exercise 23 – Fitness Ball Prone Roll-out

| START | MIDPOINT |

INSTRUCTION
- Kneel on ground with thighs vertical and arms extended forward resting on Fitness Ball with clenched fists.
- Brace and abdominals and breathe deeply.
- Breathing in, lean body forward bringing forearms to rest on ball whilst maintaining a strong and straight body from the shoulders to knees.
- Breathing out, return body to starting position by squeezing stomach muscles and drawing arms back onto fists.

Exercise Tips:
- Start with short-range movements to ensure the lower back and abdominal muscles stay firm and neutral.
- This exercise develops abdominal and shoulder strength.
- The aim of this exercise is to challenge your abdominal brace whilst extending the lever length.

THE BODY COACH

Exercise 24 – Collins-Lateral Fly™ Series – Level 1 Short Lever

| 24a. Start position | Raised position (a) | 24b. Raised position (b) |

INSTRUCTION

- Lie on side with upper body supported by the elbow (90 degrees, directly below shoulder) forearm and clenched fist with the lower body supported by the knees with legs bent.
- Lift the pelvis off the ground, eliminating the side bending by raising onto the knees, forming a straight line from the feet to head – maintaining a neutral position.
- Rise up and hold body position for three controlled breaths or 8-10 seconds – left side, then right side.

Exercise Tips:

- Do not allow hips to tilt or any stress or pain to radiate to the lower back region. Always stop the exercise if this occurs.

Exercise 25 – Collins-Lateral Fly™ Series – Level 2 Long Lever

Good alignment - straight

Poor alignment – leaning or rotated

25a. Level 2(a): Start position   **Raised position**

25b. Level 2(b) raised position   **25c. Level 2 (c) raised position**

INSTRUCTION

- Lie on side with upper body supported by the elbow (90 degrees, directly below shoulder), forearm and clenched fist. Lower body supported by feet – positioned together with legs straight.
- Lift the pelvis off the ground, eliminating the side bending by raising onto the edge of shoes or feet, forming a straight line from the feet to head – maintaining a neutral position.
- Upper arm with hand on waist.
- Level 2b. Extend arm overhead.
- Level 2c. Extend arm and raise upper leg.
- Rise up and hold body position for three controlled breaths or 8-10 seconds – left side, then right side.

Exercise Tips:

- Maintain good body alignment at all times.
- Do not allow hips to tilt or any stress or pain to radiate to the lower back region. Always stop the exercise if this occurs.
- Maintain deep breathing pattern whilst holding body position.

Exercise 26 – Collins-Lateral Fly™ Series – Level 3 Coordination Drills (weighted)

26a. Level 3(a)	Lower and raise arm

26b. Level 3(b)	Lower and raise arm with leg raised

26c. Level 3(c)	Lower and raise arm - weighted

26d. Level 3(d)	Lower and raise arm (weighted) with leg raised

INSTRUCTION

- Lie on side with upper body supported by the elbow (90 degrees, directly below shoulder), forearm and clenched fist. Lower body supported by feet – positioned together along with legs.
- Extend upper arm to open chest and raise into air.
- Lift the pelvis off the ground, eliminating the side bending by raising onto the edge of shoes or feet, forming a straight line from the feet to head – maintaining a neutral position.
- Lower and raise arm as a coordination drill (similar action to chest fly movement, but with just one arm).
- 3b. Raise upper leg to increase the challenge whilst lowering and raising arm.
- 3c. Add hand weight to exercise.
- 3d. Add hand weight to exercise with leg raised.
- Rise up and hold body position for three controlled breaths or 8-10 seconds whilst raising and lower arm. Repeat left side, then right side.

Exercise Tips:

- Maintain good body alignment at all times.
- Do not allow hips to tilt or any stress or pain to radiate to the lower back region. Always stop the exercise if this occurs.
- Maintain deep breathing pattern whilst holding body position
- Avoid any twisting or body rotation – keep body tight.
- Increase hand weight once strength levels increase, but ensure body position can be maintained.

THE BODY COACH

Exercise 27 – Advanced Oblique Twists

OPPOSITE ELBOW TO KNEE   REPEAT OPPOSITE SIDE

INSTRUCTION
- Advanced exercise only – for experienced athletes.
- Lie flat on your back with one leg straight and the other bent – feet parallel and abdominal muscles braced.
- Place hands behind the head and twist opposite elbow towards opposite knee – keeping the torso braced.
- Simultaneously straighten one leg whilst you extend the other, slightly turning the opposite elbow towards the opposite knee.
- Perform movement in a slow controlled motion whilst maintaining strong abdominal brace.
- Breathe out as you extend the leg.

Exercise Tips:
- Maintain a deep breathing pattern and a tight body position with minimal sideways movement. In which case, the torso remains stationary and small action of the arms increases the exercise intensity.
- Start with slow, controlled motion and deep breathing pattern.
- This exercise should look smooth with the athlete always in control.
- This exercise is for advanced exercisers only who can maintain pelvic and spinal alignment.

LOWER ABDOMINAL SEQUENCE

Target Area(s): Exercises 28–37: Abdominal muscles – primarily below the line on the photograph below; pelvis and hip flexors (iliopsoas).

Exercises (28–37) are focused primarily on the lower abdominal portion of the rectus abdominis and the obliques before moving on to lower back exercises. Whilst serving as one whole muscle group, the shape of the lower portion of the rectus abdominis requires exercises to be performed working from the lower region upwards, whereas most abdominal exercises work from the upper region downwards. For real benefits to occur, the waistline must be kept trim and surrounding muscles pliable. If this pelvis is tilted forwards or unstable from extra weight or weakness, this can affect your pelvic positioning and movement mechanics. In running and swimming, for instance, a weak lower abdominal region can lead to poor pelvic positioning and extra stress on other surrounding muscles, decreasing performance and leading to possible injury. A good diet and regular stretching is important for maximizing the benefits of lower abdominal exercises.

Exercise 28 – Reverse Curls

START

MIDPOINT

INSTRUCTION
- Lie on your back with knees bent and arms down by your side.
- Breathing in through the nose, then out through the mouth with pursed lips draw your navel (belly button) inwards and hold – maintaining a neutral spine.
- Maintaining a strong abdominal brace, forcefully breathe out through pursed lips - activating the lower abdominal region and raising knees towards chest keeping legs bent.
- Breathe in, slowly lower legs and reset for next repetition. Avoid relaxing abdominal brace until set is completed.

NOTE
- **Exercise Progression** – Perform reverse curls whilst holding on to end of an exercise bench with hands. Vary the angle of bench (flat to incline) to increase exercise intensity.

Exercise 29 – Touch Downs

START
Knees raised and abdominal muscles braced

MIDPOINT
Lower one leg slowly whilst maintaining neutral spine

INSTRUCTION
- Brace abdominal muscles
- Raise both legs together at 90-degree angle to hip, with toes pointed.
- Slowly, (count of "three") lower one leg maintaining a bent knee until the toes touch the ground, then return up slowly to starting position.
- Breathe out as you lower and in as you raise the leg.
- Ensure abdominal muscles are braced throughout the whole leg movement.
- Repeat with opposite leg.
- This exercise aims to build body awareness and is an extension of Exercise 11.

PROGRESSION
- Extend legs upwards from knees without straightening to increase lever length. Lower one leg with abdominal muscles braced to touch ground – then raise. Repeat opposite leg.

THE BODY COACH

Exercise 30 – Lower Leg Lifts

START

MIDPOINT – RAISE HIPS

INSTRUCTION
- Lie on your back with legs raised in the air (slightly bent) and hands placed under your buttocks – palms down.
- Breathing in through the nose, then out through the mouth with pursed lips draw your navel (belly button) inwards and hold – maintaining a neutral spine.
- Maintaining a strong abdominal brace, forcefully breathe out through pursed lips - activating the lower abdominal region and raising the hip, legs and buttocks off the ground without swinging legs or changing their length.
- Breathe in as you lower buttocks to ground.
- Over time, with good abdominal contraction you will learn to relax the upper body and focus on solely activating the abdominal region.

PROGRESSION
- Perform this exercise on a flat bench whilst holding end of the bench with both hands.
- Perform lower leg lifts on decline bench to increase intensity of exercise.

START

RAISE AND TWIST

INSTRUCTION

- Lie on your back with legs raised in the air (slightly bent) and hands placed under your buttocks – palms down.
- Breathing in through the nose, then out through the mouth with pursed lips draw your navel (belly button) inwards and hold – maintaining a neutral spine.
- Maintaining a strong abdominal brace, forcefully breathe out through pursed lips - activating the lower abdominal region and raising legs into the air twisting up to the left side, lower, then repeat on right side. Corkscrew the legs as you raise hip and buttock region off the ground.
- Breathe in as you lower buttocks to ground.
- Over time, with good abdominal contraction you will learn to relax the upper body and focus on solely activating the abdominal region.

PROGRESSION

- Perform lying on exercise bench, whilst holding end of bench with hands.
- Vary the angle (incline) of bench to increase exercise intensity.

Exercise 32 – Single Leg Stretch

START	MIDPOINT
	Raise shoulders for higher abdominal contraction

INSTRUCTION
- Lie flat on your back and extend one leg out with toe height on both feet parallel to ground.
- Catch bent leg with hands and activate abdominal brace.
- Simultaneously straighten one leg whilst you extend the other, catching the bent knee.
- Perform movement in a slow controlled motion whilst maintaining strong abdominal brace.

NOTE
- Breathe deeply in and out whilst legs continually alternate.
- Only increase speed of movement once a strong abdominal brace can be held for an extended period of time. The focus here is on quality of movement at all times.
- Raise shoulders for higher abdominal contraction.

CAPTAIN'S CHAIR DRILLS

- Lower Abdominal Sequence

SET-UP INSTRUCTION

Equipment: Captain's Chair (machines may vary)
- Rest forearms on pads, grip handles and brace abdominal muscles with the lower back supported by backing pad.
- Extend legs slightly forwards to activate abdominal and iliopsoas muscles.

Exercise 33 – Knee Raise

START | RAISE KNEES TO CHEST

INSTRUCTION
- Breathing out raise knees to chest, then slowly lower before repeating.
- Avoid legs relaxing or swinging backwards when lowering.
- Maintain slight body dish position until exercise set is complete.
- Maintain a strong abdominal brace and avoid lower back arching.

NOTE
- Start with slow controlled action – avoid swinging legs.
- Once thigh is parallel to ground, drive knees towards chest to obtain maximum benefit.

THE BODY COACH

Exercise 34 – Oblique Twist

INSTRUCTION

- As knees raise, twist knees to left side, then lower and repeat movement on the right side.
- Ensure lower back is held firmly against backing pad at all times.
- Use the abdominal muscles to drive knees towards chest whilst maintaining strong upper body position.

START

RAISE KNEES AND TWIST

Exercise 35 – Scissors

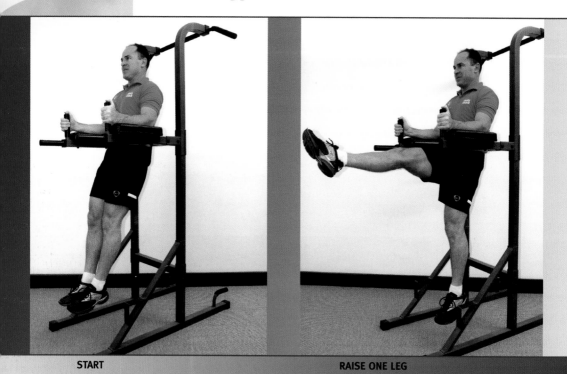

START

RAISE ONE LEG

INSTRUCTION
- Legs extended, breathe out and slowly raise the left leg until parallel to ground, then lower.
- Repeat with the right leg keeping abdominals braced at all times and lower back held firm against backing pad.

NOTE
- Movement is slow and controlled – with leg straight – muscles tense and toes pointed.

THE BODY COACH

Exercise 36 – Hip Flexion Holds: Legs Extended

START	MIDPOINT – Raise both legs without the lower back arching

INSTRUCTION
- Raise both legs and hold at approximately a 90 degree angle maintaining a strong abdominal brace until loss of form (i.e. lower back arching).
- Ensure lower back is held firmly against backing pad at all times.

NOTE
- This exercise is for ADVANCED LEVEL ATHLETES ONLY.
- Progression through previous captain's chair exercises should be mastered before attempting this exercise.
- Perform this exercise under the guidance of a coach or trainer to assist with leg holding position and ensuring lower back does not sag or arch.

Exercise 37 – Hanging Knee Raises

Equipment: High Bar

| START | MIDPOINT |

INSTRUCTION
- Grip an overhead bar and extend legs.
- Brace abdominal muscles to form a slight dish position with legs slightly forward of the body.
- Breathing out, raise knees to chest, then lower legs slowly. Aim to maintain a tight body position at all times and avoid abdominal swinging (weakness).
- Hold start position only, (dish position) to develop strength if unable to raise knees to chest.

NOTE
- A spotter may be necessary to support the lower back region of the participant to reduce swinging.
- Complete similar movements as those outlined in the Captain's Chair Exercises 33-36 in the hanging position using a partner to support the lower back region.

THE BODY COACH

LOWER BACK FOCUS

Exercise 38 – Hip Raise: Shoulder Bridge

Target Area(s): Lower back and hip region

| START | MIDPOINT – RAISE HIPS |

INSTRUCTION
- Lie flat on back with legs bent and arms by your side.
- Breathe in deeply.
- Breathe out and slowly peel the lower back off the ground and raise hips into the air.
- Breathe in at the top of the movement and reactivate abdominal muscles. Complete one full breath in and out – then in again before lowering body.
- Breathe out and lower the body in reverse motion lowering hips to ground.

NOTE
- Balance on heels to introduce more hamstrings involvement.
- Maintain square hips at all times.
- To increase the intensity of the Hip Raise, extend one leg upwards and hold as shown in Exercise 39.
- See Exercise 7 for progression on Fitness ball.

Exercise 39 – Hip Raise: One Leg Raised

Target Area(s): Lower back, hip and leg.

| START | MIDPOINT |

INSTRUCTION
- Bracing the abdominal muscles, maintain a stable pelvis whilst raising hips off the ground.
- Ensure pelvis is kept square throughout movement up and down.
- Repeat opposite leg.
- Breathe deeply throughout movement.

NOTE
- Ensure enough strength has been gained by mastering exercise 38 before attempting the one leg raise.
- Stop this exercise if you feel any lower back tension or pain.
- This movement can also be classified as a Leg Strengthening Exercise.
- See Exercise 7 for progression on Fitness ball.

THE BODY COACH

Exercise 40 – Controlled Back Raise

Target Area(s): Lower back.

| START | MIDPOINT – GENTLY RAISE SHOULDERS |

INSTRUCTION
- Lie on stomach with hands clasped behind back.
- Breathing in, contract stomach and raise upper body (chest) off floor.
- Focus on elongating the spine and rising away and up a short distance whilst maintaining braced abdominal muscles.
- Breathing out, slowly lower the chest back to the floor.

NOTE
- No tension or pain should be felt in the lower back at any time during exercise.
- Stretch lower back in between sets by lying on your back and bringing your knees to your chest.

Exercise 41 – Superman's

Target Area(s): Lower back and buttock – arms and leg coordination.

START – EXTENDED

MIDPOINT – RAISE ALTERNATE ARM AND LEG

INSTRUCTION
- Lie on stomach with arms and legs extended and forehead resting on ground.
- Brace abdominal muscles.
- Maintaining a long tight body position, simultaneously raise the left arm and right leg without overextending, and then lower as you breathe out.
- Repeat movement with right arm and left leg.

NOTE
- Raise arm and leg at similar height.
- Avoid overarching or leaning to one side.

THE BODY COACH

Exercise 42 – 4–Point Kneeling: Arm & Leg Raise

Target Area(s): Lower back, buttock, deltoid – arm and leg coordination.

| START | MIDPOINT – RAISE ARM AND OPPOSITE LEG |

INSTRUCTION
- Kneel on knees and hands and create an equal equilibrium between all four points.
- Breathing in through the nose, then out through the mouth with pursed lips draw your navel (belly button) inwards and hold – maintaining a neutral spine.
- Maintaining a strong abdominal brace, forcefully breathe out through pursed lips activating the lower abdominal region whilst simultaneously extending the leg backwards with knee slightly flexed, and opposite arm forward.
- Resisting any arching of the lower back or neck, breathe in and bring leg and arm back to starting position.
- Repeat opposite side.

NOTE
- This exercise is about timing and coordination between the arms and legs.
- Ensure exercise is performed slowly with good technique.
- Ensure head and neck are maintained in neutral position in line with your back.

Exercise 43 – Fitness Ball: Alternate Arm and Leg Raise

Target Area(s): Lower back, buttock, deltoid – arm and leg coordination.
Equipment: Fitness Ball

START – EXTENDED

MIDPOINT – RAISE ARM AND OPPOSITE LEG

INSTRUCTION
- Lying on your stomach on Fitness Ball, stabilize balance through feet – shoulder-width apart and hands.
- Brace abdominal muscles.
- Resisting any arching of the lower back or neck, simultaneously extend one arm with opposite leg until parallel with ground, and then lower.
- Repeat opposite side.

NOTE
- Maintain neutral head and neck position in line with your back at all times.

Exercise 44 – Fitness Ball Back Raise

Target Area(s): Lower back.
Equipment: Fitness Ball

| START | MIDPOINT – RAISE BODY |

INSTRUCTION

- Lying on your stomach on Fitness Ball, stabilize balance through feet, shoulder-width apart.
- Place hands behind your head.
- Maintaining a strong abdominal brace, forcefully breathe out through pursed lips activating the lower abdominal region whilst lifting chest of ball and raising upper back to a straight body position.
- Resisting any arching of the lower back or neck, breathe in and lower to starting position.

NOTE

- When first starting out, the feet may be placed against a wall for support.

Exercise 45 – Fitness Ball Ins-and-Outs

Target Area(s): Chest, shoulders, abdominals, pelvis, legs – coordination.
Equipment: Fitness Ball

START

MIDPOINT

INSTRUCTION
- Walk out and hold a strong front support position with abdominal muscles braced and shins resting on ball.
- Breathing in, draw your knees to your chest whilst raising up onto your toes.
- Breathing out, extend the legs maintaining a strong abdominal brace to resist any lower back sagging.

NOTE
- Always have a qualified coach assist with movement and support.
- Maintain neutral spine position and abdominal brace whilst breathing deeply.
- Aim to keep eye line over hands.

THE BODY COACH

Exercise 46 – Collins Functional Body Rotations™: 180 Degrees on Fitness Ball

Target Area(s): Chest, shoulders, abdominals, pelvis, legs – coordination.
Equipment: Fitness Ball

START-FINISH POSITION

ROTATION

MIDPOINT

INSTRUCTION

- Lie on ball at shoulder height across shoulder blades. Feet shoulder-width apart, arms extended to the side.
- Keeping arms extended rotate to the left side, maintaining strong feel with the ball across the chest to maintain ball control.

NOTE

- Rotating to the left moves the ball across to the right side. As a result, whilst rotating lift the left leg underneath the right as you roll you're your stomach and extend it out to control movement (Midpoint photo).
- Reverse movement by rotating arms and bringing left leg back under to return onto your back.
- Repeat movement three times on the left side, and then repeat in the opposite direction turning the arms to the right as well as lifting and moving the right leg into position.
- This exercise develops muscle coordination between the upper and lower body through the body's core. It requires full concentration and awareness for total muscle activation and control.

PROGRESSION

- Collins 360-degree functional body rotation™ on fitness ball – to the left and right sides in a straight line.

NOTE

- Perform exercises using opposite arms or leg, if required.
- Refer to chapter 9 for establishing repetitions (reps) and sets.

ABDOMINAL and LOWER BACK EXERCISE SUMMARY

10. Abdominal Bracing – Supine Position	11a – Abdominal Bracing: Supine Position (Level 1)	11b – Abdominal Bracing: Supine Position (Level 2)

Perform__sets,__reps	Perform__sets,__reps	Perform__sets,__reps

11c – Abdominal Bracing: Supine Position (Level 3)	12 – Abdominal Bracing: Prone Position	13. Abdominal Slide
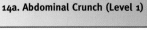		
Perform__sets,__reps	Hold for__secs,__times	Perform__sets,__reps

14a. Abdominal Crunch (Level 1)	14b. Abdominal Crunch (Level 2)	14c. Abdominal Crunch (Level 3)

Perform__sets,__reps	Perform__sets,__reps	Perform__sets,__reps

15. Medicine Ball Coordination Crunch	16a. Fitness Ball Abdominal Crunch (Level 1)	16b. Fitness Ball Abdominal Crunch (Level 2)

Perform__sets,__reps	Perform__sets,__reps	Perform__sets,__reps

16c. Fitness Ball Abdominal Crunch (Level 3)

Perform__sets,__reps

16d. Fitness Ball Abdominal Crunch (Level 4)

Perform__sets,__reps

16e. Fitness Ball Abdominal Crunch (Level 5)

Perform__sets,__reps

17. The Hundred Drill

Perform__sets,__reps

18. Medicine Ball Raise

Perform__sets,__reps

19. Lateral Side Raises

Perform__sets,__reps

20a. Abdominal Oblique (Level 1)

Perform__sets,__reps

20b. Abdominal Oblique (Level 2)

Perform__sets,__reps

20c. Abdominal Oblique (Level 3)

Perform__sets,__reps

20d. Abdominal Oblique (Level 4)

Perform__sets,__reps

20e. Abdominal Oblique (Level 5)

Perform__sets,__reps

20f. Abdominal Oblique (Level 6)

Perform__sets,__reps

THE BODY COACH

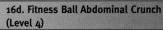

21. Medicine Ball Twist

Perform__sets,__reps

22a. Fitness Ball Oblique Twist

Perform__sets,__reps

22b. Fitness Ball Oblique Twist

Perform__sets,__reps

23. Fitness Ball Prone Roll-out

Perform__sets,__reps

24a. Collins Lateral Fly™ Series (Level 1)

Perform__sets,__reps

24b. Collins lateral Fly™ Series (Level 1)

Perform__sets,__reps

25a. Collins Lateral Fly™ Series (Level 2)

Perform__sets,__reps

25b. Collins Lateral Fly™ Series (Level 2)

Perform__sets,__reps

25c. Collins Lateral Fly™ Series (Level 2)

Perform__sets,__reps

26a. Collins Lateral Fly™ Series (Level 3)

Perform__sets,__reps

26b. Collins Lateral Fly™ Series (Level 3)

Perform__sets,__reps

26c. Collins Lateral Fly™ Series (Level 3)

Perform__sets,__reps

26d. Collins Lateral Fly™ Series (Level 3)

Perform__sets,__reps

27. Advanced Oblique Twists

Perform__sets,__reps

28. Reverse Curls

Perform__sets,__reps

29. Touch Downs

Perform__sets,__reps

30. Lower Leg Lifts

Perform__sets,__reps

31. Lower Abdominal Corkscrew

Perform__sets,__reps

32. Single Leg Stretch

Perform__sets,__reps

33. Knee Raise

Perform__sets,__reps

34. Oblique Twist

Perform__sets,__reps

35. Scissors

Perform__sets,__reps

36. Hip Flexion Holds

Perform__sets,__reps

37. Hanging Knee Raises

Perform__sets,__reps

38. Hip Raise

Perform__sets,__reps

39. Hip Raise

Perform__sets,__reps

40. Controlled Back Raise

Perform__sets,__reps

41. Superman's

Perform__sets,__reps

42. 4-Point Kneeling

Perform__sets,__reps

43. Fitness Ball Alternate Leg and Arm Raise

Perform__sets,__reps

44. Fitness Ball Back Raise

Perform__sets,__reps

45. Fitness Ball Ins-and-Outs

Perform__sets,__reps

46. Collins Functional Body Rotations

Perform__sets,__reps

Chapter 5

Leg and Hip Muscles

The muscles involved while performing strength exercises for the legs and hip are namely the gluteal region, quadriceps, hamstrings and calves:

GLUTEAL REGION
Often referred to as the buttock region, the primary function is hip extension in unison with the hip stabilizers important in all lower body movements.

QUADRICEPS
This is the large group of muscles on the front of the upper leg, often referred to as the thighs – starting at the hip joint and ending at the knee joint. Their primary function is to flex the hip and extend the knee, very important in walking, running, jumping, climbing and pedalling a bike.

HAMSTRINGS
This is the group of muscles on the backside of the leg, running from the hip joint to the knee joint. Their primary function is to facilitate flexion of legs, medial and lateral rotation, important for walking, running and jumping.

CALVES
The groups of muscles further down the back of the leg running from the backside of the knee to the Achilles tendon. They help us to extend our foot at the ankle and flex the toes, which in turn help us in walking, running, pedalling a bike and jumping.

The following exercises are designed to help strengthen the legs, stabilize the hip, knee and ankle joints and improve coordination and range of motion.

Exercise 47 – Wall-Sits

Target Area(s): Legs (thigh) and abdominal muscles.

HOLD AT 110 DEGREE ANGLE

Progression 1
Lower body towards 90-degree leg angle and hold (never lower)

PROGRESSION 2
Add a weight – i.e. Medicine Ball

INSTRUCTION
- Stand against a wall then take feet approximately 40-60 cm forward.
- Slightly bend the knees and hold for 20-60 seconds or more.
- Maintain a strong abdominal brace and deep breathing pattern throughout.
- Lower angle of legs and hold longer length of time to increase intensity.
- This exercise is isometric in nature and needs to be worked at various angles.
- Vary the angle of the legs but never below 90-degree knee angle as stress increases on the knees.

PROGRESSION
- To increase the intensity of the exercise hold a Medicine Ball straight out with your arms.
- This introduces isometric strengthening of the arms, shoulders and abdominal region, whilst working the legs.

THE BODY COACH

Exercise 48 – Lateral Leg Lifts

Target Area(s): Hip abductors. Helps create muscular balance of the hip region for better pelvic stability.

| START | MIDPOINT –
Keep heel as the highest point |

INSTRUCTION
- Lie on side of body with legs together and upper arm forward supporting the weight of the body.
- Breathing in, tighten thigh, heel high, toes pointing downwards and pulled back toward shins.
- Breathing out, slowly raise your upper leg without twisting your hips.
- Breathe in and lower in a controlled motion.
- Repeat opposite leg.

NOTE
- Ensure body is straight and slightly tilted forward to allow effective strengthening of hip abductors.
- Leaning back or with the toes upwards changes the target muscle group, so ensure heels are the highest point.
- The lateral leg lift is a good warm-up exercise for all athletes that can be followed by Iliotibial band (ITB) stretches to help release muscular tension of the pelvic region.
- See Exercise 49 for progression with resistance.

Exercise 49 – Lateral Leg Lifts: Resisted

Target Area(s): Hip abductors.
Equipment: Resistance Band

| START | MIDPOINT |

INSTRUCTION
- Lie on side of body with resistance band around legs and upper arm forward supporting the weight of the body (see exercise 48).
- Raise upper leg keeping the heel as the highest point, then lower.
- Repeat opposite leg.

NOTE
- Raise and lower upper leg, keeping heel as highest point and toes facing down at all times – keep upper body slightly forwards.
- This exercise can also be performed standing (see Exercise 50)

THE BODY COACH

Exercise 50 – Standing Lateral Leg Lifts (Resisted)

Target Area(s): Hip abductors.
Equipment: Resistance Band

START   MIDPOINT

INSTRUCTION
- Stand tall next to bench, pole or chair with resistance band attached around outside leg.
- On inside foot raise onto toes to allow free flow movement of opposite leg.
- Bracing abdominals, breathe out as you raise outside leg away from body leading with the heel, keeping toes turned slightly inwards towards body.
- Maintain upright body position.
- Breathe in and return leg to starting point.
- Repeat opposite leg.

NOTE
- Maintain heel as furthest point with toes pulled back and down to ensure targeting hip abductors.

Exercise 51 – Adductor Leg Lifts

Target Area(s): Hip adductors.

START MIDPOINT

INSTRUCTION
- Lie of side on body with upper leg bent and forward of lower extended leg.
- Breathe in, tighten thigh of extended leg.
- Breathe out and raise lower leg up, keeping toes pulled back towards shins, then lower leg.
- Repeat opposite leg.

NOTE
- Maintain straight body and leg position throughout movement to target hip adductors.

Exercise 52 – Pelvic Lifts

Target Area(s): Hip abductors; Quadratus lumborum.

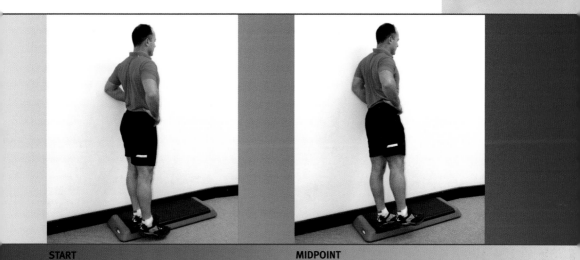

START   MIDPOINT

INSTRUCTION
- Stand with one foot on step (stable block or bench), the outside foot free.
- Rest hands on wall or chair for support and brace abdominal muscles.
- In a controlled manner, slowly raise and lower the free leg focusing on pelvic lift and lowering – using the hip abductors.
- All the action occurs from the pelvic region.
- Repeat opposite leg.

NOTE
- Hip abductors provide core-strength and stability for the leg kick.
- They also help stabilize the hip when walking, lunging and climbing stairs.
- Movement range is small so make conscious effort to stabilize pelvis and control movement at all times.

Exercise 53 – Standing Heel Raises

Target Area(s): Calves.

| START | MIDPOINT – ON TOES |

INSTRUCTION
- Stand tall, feet shoulder-width apart, hands on hips or resting on support.
- Align feet and knees to establish a foot arch in both feet.
- Slowly raise up onto toes, then lower.

VARIATION
- Step or Bench: Stand with ball of foot off edge of step and raise and lower heels to strengthen calves and ankles.

NOTE
- In-time with one's breath, slowly breathe out as you raise onto your toes.
- Breathe in whilst you lower, in a controlled motion.

THE BODY COACH

Exercise 54 – Balance Calf-Raise

Target Area(s): Calves, foot and ankle stability.

START

MIDPOINT
Rise onto toes maintaining balance

INSTRUCTION
- Stand with one leg raised at 90 degrees at the hip off the ground to add intensity to the exercise (from Exercise 53).
- Place hands on hips or extended out to side for balance.
- Align supporting foot and knee to establish a foot arch.
- Slowly rise up onto toes, maintaining balance, then lower.
- Repeat opposite leg.

NOTE
- Brace abdominal muscles to assist in maintaining balance.
- Use support-base such as chair until balance is improved when first starting out.

Exercise 55 – Resistance Band Kickback

Target Area(s): Gluteal (buttocks); Hamstrings & Abdominals (isometrically).
Equipment: Resistance Band

START   MIDPOINT

INSTRUCTION
- Attach resistance band around pole, bench or chair.
- Stand tall on one leg with resistance band attached to opposed leg.
- Pull toes up towards shins (dorsi flex).
- Raise up onto toes of free leg to allow for effective range of motion of the other leg.
- Bracing abdominals, breathe out as you kick the leg backwards away from body, then return.
- Repeat opposite leg.

NOTE
- Maintain strong abdominal brace to avoid lower back arching.
- Keep toes dorsi-flexed at all times throughout movement.
- Progress to cable machine with ankle attachment.

THE BODY COACH

Exercise 56 – Fitness Ball Kickbacks

Target Area(s): Gluteal (buttocks); Hamstrings (isometrically).
Equipment: Fitness Ball

START   MIDPOINT

INSTRUCTION
- Lie over Fitness Ball on stomach with hands and feet on ground.
- Brace abdominal muscles and pull toes back towards shins (dorsi-flex).
- Breathing out, extend one leg up until parallel to ground.
- Maintain square pelvis, keep foot vertical and toes dorsi-flexed.
- Continue with short pulses up and down to target rear of upper leg and buttocks.
- Repeat opposite leg.

NOTE
- Avoid turning foot out to side. Maintain straight body alignment.
- To strengthen gluteal (buttock) region bend leg and pulse foot up in small movements without losing body position or twisting to the side.

Exercise 57 – Medicine Ball Leg Curls

Target Area(s): Hamstrings.
Equipment: Medicine Ball

1. START – ROLL DOWN LEGS

2.

3. MIDPOINT – KICK AND CATCH

4.

INSTRUCTION

- Lie on your stomach with feet together with partner standing at shoulder level facing towards your feet, holding Medicine Ball in hands in a semi-squat position.
- The partner rolls the ball down the back of your legs, as it reaches towards your calf region curl your legs and kick the Medicine Ball back up to your partner who catches it and repeats the drill.

NOTE

- If both legs are even in strength, the ball should return straight when curled back. An imbalance in leg strength will lead to the ball being kicked to the side. The partner should be conscious at all times with both hands raised ready to catch the Medicine Ball. If athlete has strong kick, the partner may need to move further away from partner for more effective catch.

THE BODY COACH

SQUAT SERIES

Exercise 58 – Body Weight Squat (a–b)

Target Area(s): Legs, hip and buttocks.
Refer to Chapter 1 for correct body alignment

58a. START

MIDPOINT
GOOD ALIGNMENT

INSTRUCTION
- Stand with feet shoulder-width apart, arms extended forward and parallel with ground.
- Establish foot arch, knee and hip alignment.
- Breathe in; bend the knees and lower body maintaining good body alignment to 90 degree leg angle.
- Maintain neutral balance and alignment through ears, shoulder, knees and feet.
- Breathe out and rise upwards to complete one repetition.

NOTE
- Refer to chapter 1 for foot arch awareness and leg alignment to master the squat exercise.
- Perform the exercise slow and controlled (ie. 2 secs up and 2 secs down) focusing on good alignment and body position.
- The body weight squat is a great warm-up exercise before sport and physical activity.

58b. Supported Squat

HOLD POLE FOR SUPPORT   SLIDE HANDS DOWN POLE FOR SUPPORT

INSTRUCTION

- Use pole, wall or doorframe to perfect the squat movement pattern.
- Maintain normal squat position using hands to support movement until body is aligned and balanced. Then move away from pole and repeat movement 58a.
- Keep head close to pole when lowering.
- Push hips backwards whilst maintaining upright shoulder and head position.
- Ensure knees aligned over toes (without rolling in).

NOTE

- Apply principles for feet and leg alignment (Chapter 1).
- This exercise is a great way to warm-up muscles prior to exercising, developing muscle synergy, timing and range of motion.
- See exercise 63 to progress to a single leg (supported) squat once strength allows.

Exercise 59 – Fitness Ball Wall Squat

Target Area(s): Legs, hip and buttocks.
Equipment: Fitness Ball

START   MIDPOINT

INSTRUCTION
- Stand tall, feet shoulder-width apart.
- Position Fitness Ball behind mid-back and against wall.
- Extend both arms forward.
- Align feet and knees for natural foot arch.
- Breathing-in, slowly lower body towards ground by bending the knees and rolling buttocks under Fitness Ball – keeping knees forward over toes – with ball rolling to shoulder height.
- Breathe out and return to upright starting position.
- Perform the exercise slow and controlled (ie. 2 secs up and 2 secs down) focusing on good alignment and body position.

NOTE
- See Good Alignment in Exercise 58 (Side View) to ensure similar movement occurs and that you are not sitting backwards.
- Maintain knees over toes, shoulders over knees.

Exercise 60 – Weighted Dumbbell Squat

Target Area(s): Legs, hip and buttocks.
Equipment: Hand Weight

START   LOWERED

INSTRUCTION
- Stand with feet shoulder-width apart, arms extended downwards with light dumbbell held in hands (longways).
- Align feet and knees for natural foot arch.
- Breathe in whilst simultaneously bending the hip, knee and ankles and lowering the body until dumbbell comes near or touches the ground.
- Maintain neutral balance through shoulder, knees and feet.
- Keep arms straight at all times and movement slow and controlled.
- Breathe out and rise upwards to complete one repetition.

NOTE
- Apply principles in chapter 1 for feet and leg alignment.
- Avoid leaning forward – Keep hand weight still with arms extended down and perform normal squat movement.
- In most instances, the dumbbell will touch the ground to show end range of movement.

THE BODY COACH

Exercise 61 – Weighted Medicine Ball Squat

Target Area(s): Legs, hip and buttocks.
Equipment: Medicine Ball

START   MIDPOINT

INSTRUCTION
- Stand with feet shoulder-width apart, arms bent holding Medicine Ball against chest.
- Align feet and knees for natural foot arch.
- Breathe in whilst simultaneously bending the hip, knee and ankles and lowering the body towards 90 degree knee angle.
- Maintain neutral balance through shoulder, knees and feet.
- Breathe out and rise upwards to complete one repetition.

NOTE
- Ensure proper squat mechanics are maintained – see Exercise 58.
- Progress to Exercise 62.

Exercise 62 – Medicine Ball Push-Press

Target Area(s): Legs, hip and buttocks (and arms)
Equipment: Medicine Ball

START   MIDPOINT

INSTRUCTION
- Stand with feet shoulder-width apart, arms bent holding Medicine Ball against chest.
- Align feet and knees for natural foot arch.
- Breathe in whilst simultaneously bending the hip, knee and ankles and lowering the body towards 90 degree knee angle.
- Maintain neutral balance through shoulder, knees and feet.
- Breathe out and raise upwards extending the arms overhead.
- Keep abdominals braced, back flat and body long.
- Breathe in as you lower to complete one repetition.

NOTE
- Ensure proper squat mechanics are maintained.
- Progress to squat with medicine ball release in open area (i.e., field).

THE BODY COACH

Exercise 63 – Assisted Single Leg Squat

Target Area(s): Legs, hip and buttocks
Equipment: Wall support (or pole)

START   MIDPOINT

INSTRUCTION
- Stand tall next to wall, pole or doorframe for support.
- Grip wall with hands and extend one leg forward.
- Align feet and knees for natural foot arch.
- Breathe in whilst simultaneously bending the hip, knee and ankles and lowering the body until 90 degree knee angle sliding hands down pole support (if required).
- Breathing out raise up to start position.
- Maintain neutral balance through shoulder, knees and feet.
- Repeat opposite leg.

NOTE
- Use hands as required to assist with movement. Lessen this assistance as you become stronger.
- Be conscious at all times of maintaining correct body position.
- Start with small squat leg movement (angle) only, and then gradually add depth to 90-degrees as you become stronger.
- Progress to single leg squat without assistance.

Exercise 64 – Stationary Leg Lunge

Target Area(s): Legs, hip and buttocks.

START   MIDPOINT

INSTRUCTION
- Stand tall and extend one leg forward – with rear leg resting on toes and placing hands on hips.
- Breathing in, slowly lower your body by bending your knees – keeping your knees aligned over your toes and making sure the rear knee is well clear of the front heel.
- As legs reach 90 degrees or the rear knee approximately 5 cm from the ground, breathe out and rise up to the upright starting position.
- Repeat desired repetitions on one leg, and then repeat with other leg forward.

NOTE
- Be conscious at all times of maintaining correct body alignment.
- The hips should be square at all times when lowering and raising and the lower back should not arch.
- This applies to all lunge variations from Exercises 64-67.

THE BODY COACH

Exercise 65 – Alternate Leg Lunge Variations (a–d)

Target Area(s): Legs, hip and buttocks

65a. START   MIDPOINT

INSTRUCTION
- Stand tall, feet together hands on hips.
- Breathing in, step forward (lunge) and slowly lower your body by bending your knees – keeping your knees aligned over your toes.
- As your rear knee reaches approximately 5 cm from the ground, breath out through pursed lips, activating a strong abdominal brace, and push back up to the upright starting position.
- Repeat desired repetitions on one leg, and then the other.

NOTE
- Keep tall through the chest and aim to make movement flow efficiently.
- Keep knee aligned over toe.
- Maintain a strong pelvic position parallel to ground at all times without letting the pelvis tilt or lower on one side with all exercises 65a-d.

PROGRESSION OF INTENSITY

65b. Walking Lunge
Lunge forward in a continuous fluent walking lunge motion, keeping hips square, abdominals braced, chest tall and body upright.

65c. Stair Walking
Stand tall in front of stair well and brace abdominal muscles. Depending on age and limb length, lunge upstairs between 2-4 steps at a time. Aim to keep hips square and avoid leaning forward. Forcefully breathe out with each step.

65d. Raised Lunge – rear foot on chair or bench
Stand in Forward Lunge position with rear foot pointed and resting on solid stable chair. With hands on hips for balance, breathe in as you lower rear knee towards the ground as low as possible without touching ground. (NOTE: Depth is important to maximize strength potential.) Breathe out as you rise up again. Complete set and repeat with opposite leg. Ensure hips stay square and knee line is maintained over forward foot at all times.

65d. START

MIDPOINT – Lower knee, then raise up

THE BODY COACH

Exercise 66 – Multi-Directional Lunge Series

Target Area(s): Legs, hip and buttocks; abdominals (isometrically); motor-coordination.

Equipment: Markers

INSTRUCTION
- Set up markers in a semi-circular arch one-lunge step away from body.
- Stand tall hands on hips in center.
- Breathe in and lunge forward keeping upper body vertical to forward marker then push back breathing out.
- Perform one set using the same leg, lunging out and back to each marker – forward; 45 degree angle forward; sideways; back at 45 degree angle; backwards.
- Repeat opposite leg by facing the opposite direction.

NOTE
- Maintain a strong pelvic position parallel to ground at all times without letting the pelvis drop or lower on one side.
- This exercise requires a strong abdominal brace and good body position.
- This exercise can be used as a test of coordination and is good for activities that require multi-directional changes (agility) and dynamic warm-up and stretching.
- A call by the coach can be made to a particular marker to add variety and challenge to the exercise.

START AND RETURN POSITION

LUNGE FORWARD, then back

LUNGE 45-DEGREES

LUNGE SIDEWAYS

LUNGE BACKWARDS 45-degrees

LUNGE BACKWARDS

THE BODY COACH

Exercise 67 – Single-Leg Drives

Target Area(s): Legs, hip and buttocks; abdominals (isometrically).
Equipment: Solid stable bench or chair

START   MIDPOINT

INSTRUCTION
- Stand in forward lunge position with one foot resting up on bench.
- Brace abdominal muscles and use hands for balance.
- Keeping pelvis square, breathe out as your drive up to straighten forward leg.
- Breath-in and lower in a controlled motion – keeping upper body leaning slightly forward to maintain tension on forward leg.
- Repeat on opposite leg.

NOTE
- Ensure good ankle, knee, hip and body alignment is maintained when raising and lowering the body.
- Place bench next to wall to allow for added support using hands (if required).

Exercise 68 – Skipping

Target Area(s): Calves, abdominals (isometrically), shoulder and upper back; motor-coordination.
Equipment: Skipping Rope

INSTRUCTION
- Hold skipping rope in both hands and brace abdominals.
- Keep upper arms (elbow to shoulder) close to the body in a relaxed state whilst rotating the hands to jump rope.
- Maintain deep breathing pattern, strong core and relaxed flowing feeling.
- Increase speed and alternate legs as your quality improves.

NOTE
- Skipping requires practice.
- Initially, coordination and timing may not be with you, although, with time and practice you will become very competent.

Exercise 69 – Single-Leg Bow

Target Area(s): Legs, hip and buttocks and lower back

START

MIDPOINT
Keep back flat, pelvis square and knee aligned over toes as you slowly lower by simultaneously bending at the hip and knee until parallel to ground, then rising

INSTRUCTION
- Stand on one leg and bend the other leg behind the body.
- Extend arms down by side with clenched fists and brace abdominal muscles.
- Keeping pelvis square simultaneously bend the forward leg and lean upper body forward until chest is parallel to ground.
- Maintain neutral head position in line with body throughout movement and deep breathing pattern – in as you lower and out as you rise.
- Complete set and repeat on opposite leg.

NOTE
- Avoid pelvis dropping, lower back arching or leaning to one side.
- Ensure good ankle, knee, hip and body alignment is maintained when raising and lowering the body.
- Add light hand weights to the drill once you become competent.

Exercise 70 – Hamstrings Bridge (a–b)

Target Area(s): Hamstrings, hip and lower back

| 70a. START | MIDPOINT |

| 70b. START (Single Leg) | MIDPOINT |

INSTRUCTION
- Lie on back with knees bent and arms extended out to side.
- 70a. Raise up onto heels with feet close together.
- 70b. Single Leg: Raise up onto heels and rest one leg across the other.
- Breathing out, slowly raise hips until body is aligned.
- Breath in and lower body keeping hips square.

NOTE
- 70b. Complete set and repeat on opposite leg.
- Avoid pelvis dropping, lower back arching or leaning to one side.

THE BODY COACH

LEG STRENGTHENING EXERCISES

47. Wall-sits

48. Lateral Leg Lifts

49. Lateral Leg Lifts - resisted

Perform__sets,__reps

Perform__sets,__reps

Perform__sets,__reps

50. Standing Lateral Leg Lifts - resisted

51. Adductor Lateral Leg Lifts

52. Pelvic Lifts

Perform__sets,__reps

Perform__sets,__reps

Perform__sets,__reps

53. Standing Heel Raises

54. Balance Calf Raise

55. Resistance Band Kickbacks

Perform__sets,__reps

Perform__sets,__reps

Perform__sets,__reps

56. Fitness Ball Kickbacks

Perform__sets,__reps

57. Medicine Ball Leg Curls

Perform__sets,__reps

58a. Body Weight Squat

Perform__sets,__reps

58b. Body weight squat supported

Perform__sets,__reps

59. Fitness Ball Wall Squat

Perform__sets,__reps

60. Weighted Dumbbell Squat

Perform__sets,__reps

61. Medicine Ball Squat

Perform__sets,__reps

62. Medicine Ball Push Press

Perform__sets,__reps

63. Assisted Single Leg Squat

Perform__sets,__reps

THE BODY COACH

64. Stationary Leg Lunge

Perform__sets,__reps

65a. Alternate Leg Lunge

Perform__sets,__reps

65d. Raised Lunge

Perform__sets,__reps

66. Multi-directional Lunges

Perform__sets,__reps

67. Single Leg Drives

Perform__sets,__reps

68. Skipping

Perform__sets,__reps

69. Single Leg Bow

Perform__sets,__reps

70a. Hamstrings Bridge

Perform__sets,__reps

70a. Hamstrings Bridge

Perform__sets,__reps

NOTE
- Perform exercises using opposite leg, if required.
- Refer to chapter 9 for establishing repetitions (reps) and sets.

CORE STRENGTH

Chapter 6

Back and Arm Muscles

The following exercises target both the back and arm muscles. Exercises include movement through the shoulder blades, shoulder girdle, elbow and wrist joints. The primary muscles used include:

- **Latissimus dorsi** – Large muscles of the mid-back. When properly trained they give the back a nice V shape, making the waist appear smaller. Exercise examples include pull-ups, chin-ups and pull downs.

- **Rhomboids** – Muscles in the middle of the upper back between the shoulder blades. They're worked during chin-ups and other moves that bring the shoulder blades together.

- **Trapezius** – Upper portion of the back, sometimes referred to as 'traps.' The upper trapezius is the muscle running from the back of the neck to the shoulder.

- **Deltoids** – The cap of the shoulder. This muscle has three parts, anterior deltoid (the front), medial deltoid (the middle), and posterior deltoid (the rear). Different movements target the different heads. The anterior deltoid is worked with push-ups and front dumbbell raises. Standing lateral (side) dumbbell raises target the medial deltoid. Rear dumbbell raises or reverse flies (lying face down on a bench or fitness ball) target the posterior deltoid. Exercises for the shoulder region will be described in detail in Chapter 8.

- **Biceps** – The front of the upper arm. The best moves are biceps curls with resistance bands as well as other pulling movements like reverse grip chin-ups.

- **Triceps** – The back of the upper arm. Exercises include pushing movements like push-ups and arm dips described in more detail in Chapter 7.

Exercise 71 – Weighted Arm Extension

Target Area(s): Back and deep abdominal muscles.
Equipment: Medicine Ball

START   MIDPOINT

INSTRUCTION
- Lie on your back with knees bent.
- Raise both arms towards the ceiling holding a weighted Rebound Medicine Ball™.
- Breathing in, slowly lower the arms from overhead in an arch motion, resisting any arching of the lower back.
- As you reach the end phase of arm motion, forcefully breathe out and slowly raise arms upwards towards the ceiling.

NOTE
- Excellent exercise for building good body awareness, improving lower back strength and abdominal bracing.
- Count 3 seconds down, 3 seconds up using light weight.
- Maintain strong abdominal brace and deep breathing pattern.

THE BODY COACH

Exercise 72 – Prone Upper Back Drills (a-c)

Target Area(s): Upper back, shoulder region (posterior) and Scapula.
Equipment: Hand Weights (70c. Fitness Ball)

72a. SLIGHTLY BENT ARMS   **72b. THUMBS RAISED**

INSTRUCTION
- Lie on your stomach, brace abdominals and extend arms out to side.
- In the initial strength development, support forehead with rolled towel to maintain good head and neck alignment with the body.
- 72a. Slightly bend arms, palms facing down - raise hands and arms off ground and hold isometrically for short period (add weight to hands as shown as strength improves).
- 72b. Hold arms straight and turn thumbs upwards. Raise hands and arms off ground and hold isometrically for short period (as shown).
- Ensure head and neck alignment is maintained at all times with the rest of the body for the development of good posture.

NOTE
- Maintain deep breathing pattern.
- Hold each position for 5-10 seconds or more. Repeat 5-10 times.
- Add light dumbbells to hands to increase intensity (as shown above).
- Kayaking is an excellent way to build muscular endurance in this area.

72c. FITNESS BALL REVERSE FLYES

72c. HEAD NEUTRAL, ARMS SLIGHTLY BENT   **EXTEND ARMS UP AND OUT**

INSTRUCTION
- Lie over Fitness Ball with head held neutral, arms extended down and slightly bent with light dumbbells in hand.
- Breathing out, slowly extend arms up and out away from body keeping back and head aligned.
- Breathe in and lower arms keeping abdominal muscles braced.

NOTE
- Keep arms slightly bent and wrists straight at all times.
- This exercise also strengthen rear deltoids (shoulders): Chapter 8.

THE BODY COACH

Exercise 73 – Single Arm Pull-Downs

Target Area(s): Back and abdominal muscles – Motor-coordination and breathing.
Equipment: Resistance Band (or cable)

START   MIDPOINT

INSTRUCTION
- Stand tall, brace abdominal muscles with one arm forward of the body holding resistance band (or cable).
- Breathing out pull band/cable down towards thigh.
- Breathe in and extend arm back up to starting position.
- Ensure long body position is maintained at all times.
- Keep wrist and arm straight at all times.
- Repeat movement with opposite arm.

VARIATION
- Vary body angle to resistance band (i.e. angle body forward) and move into forward lunge stance.
- Introduce loaded cable machine to increase resistance both down and up.

Exercise 74 – Double Arm Pull-Downs (a-c)

Target Area(s): Back and abdominal muscles – Motor-coordination & Balance.
Equipment: Resistance Band (or cable)

| 74a. START | 74a. MIDPOINT | 74b. VARIATION | ONE LEG RAISED FORWARD | 74c. VARIATION | ONE KNEE FLEXED |

INSTRUCTION
- 74a. Stand with feet shoulder-width apart, arms extended forward holding resistance bands.
- Establish natural foot arch and brace abdominals.
- Breathing out pull both arms down past thighs.
- Breathe in and return to starting position.

74b. Repeat movement with one leg forward and raised.
- The torso is held upright with balancing leg slightly bent.

74c. Repeat movement with knee bent and raised behind body.
- The torso is held slightly forward with balancing leg slightly bent.

NOTE
- Maintain good body alignment at all times by keeping abdominal muscles braced.

THE BODY COACH

Exercise 75 – Wide-Grip Pull-Ups: 45-Degree

Target Area(s): Back, arms and abdominal muscles.
Equipment: Bar, solid table (or smith machine)

STARTING POSITION   **MIDPOINT**

INSTRUCTION
- Using an adjustable bar (such as Smith Machine) or solid and stable table, adapt a wide overhand grip (thumbs inward), arms extended, keeping the body tight.
- Breathe out as you pull your body up towards the bar (or table), hold briefly then breathe in as you lower – keeping the body tight at all times.
- Use bent legs or straight legs to increase intensity of the exercise

NOTE
- Bend the knees to shorten the body lever length and reduce the intensity, whilst extending the legs increases the level length and the demand.
- A coach must help support your body by holding underneath your back and assisting with the movement until one becomes stronger.
- Change grips – wide or narrow for variation.
- Ensure head and neck alignment is maintained at all times with the rest of the body for the development of good posture.

Exercise 76 – Supine Biceps Pull-Ups: 45-Degree

Target Area(s): Back, arms (biceps) and abdominal muscles.
Equipment: Table or smith machine

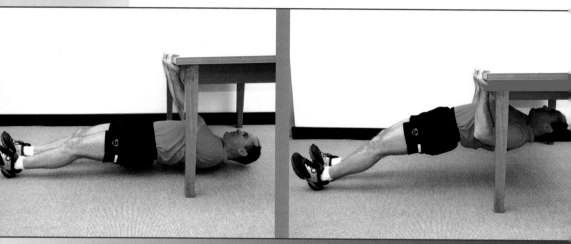

STARTING POSITION   MIDPOINT

INSTRUCTION
- Using an adjustable bar (such as Smith Machine) or solid and stable table, adapt a reverse grip (thumbs outward) shoulder width apart, maintaining a tight body position.
- Breathe out as you pull up towards the bar, keeping your body upright until your chin reaches the bar, hold briefly then breathe in as you lower.

NOTE
- Bend the knees to shorten the body lever length and reduce the intensity, whilst extending the legs increases the level length and the demand.
- Ensure head and neck alignment is maintained at all times with the rest of the body for the development of good posture.
- A coach must help support your body by holding underneath your back and assisting with the movement until you become stronger.

THE BODY COACH

Exercise 77 – Reverse Grip Chin-Ups (a-b)

Target Area(s): Back, arms (biceps) and abdominal muscles.
Equipment: High Bar (and bench)

77a. STARTING POSITION   **MIDPOINT**

INSTRUCTION
- On a high bar, adapt a reverse grip (thumbs outward) with hands and elbows parallel and slightly bent.
- Breathe out as you pull up towards the bar, keeping your body upright until your chin reaches the bar, hold briefly then breathe in as you lower.
- Maintain muscle control and smooth flow when pulling up and lowering down.

77b. SELF-SPOTTING APPROACH

To assist in the development of performing a biceps pull-up, a bench is placed under the feet. With arms extended holding your bodyweight, position one foot on the bench provided. In raising the body, keeping the tension on the arms – slowly add the pressure of the foot to the bench to assist in raising the body.

77b. STARTING POSITION

MIDPOINT –
Raise body with leg assistance

NOTE
- Focus on the tension on the arms with the assistance of the leg being secondary.
- This approach helps maintain good posture (form), whilst building strength and confidence.
- Over time as you become stronger the assistance of the leg is reduced or removed from the exercise.

THE BODY COACH

Exercise 78 – Wide-Grip Chin-Ups (a-b)

Target Area(s): Back, arms and abdominal muscles.
Equipment: High Bar (and bench)

78a. STARTING POSITION   MIDPOINT

INSTRUCTION
- On a high bar, adapt a wide overhand grip (thumbs inward), arms extended.
- Breathe out as you pull up towards the bar, keeping your body upright until your chin reaches the bar. Hold briefly, then breathe in as you lower.
- Your grip should be wide enough to maintain the focus on the back muscles.
- Change width of hand grip for variation in future training sessions as you become stronger.

NOTE
- The midpoint can also be held for set periods of time for those wanting to gain isometric core strength.

78b. SELF-SPOTTING APPROACH

To assist in the development of performing a wide-grip pull-up, a bench is placed under the feet. With arms extended holding your bodyweight, position one foot on the bench provided. In raising the body, keeping the tension on the arms – slowly add the pressure of the foot to the bench to assist in raising the body.

78b. STARTING POSITION

MIDPOINT –
Raise body with leg assistance

NOTE
- Focus on the tension on the arms with the assistance of the leg being secondary.
- This approach helps maintain good posture (form), whilst building strength and confidence.
- Over time as you become stronger the assistance of the leg is reduced or removed from the exercise.

THE BODY COACH

Exercise 79 – Close Grip Pull-Ups

Target Area(s): Back, arms and abdominal muscles.
Equipment: High Bar (and bench)

79a. STARTING POSITION   MIDPOINT

INSTRUCTION
- Stand with the bar running through the line of sight.
- Reach up and grab bar, one hand in front of the other, with palms facing each another.
- Breathe out as you pull up to cross left side of the bar, hold briefly then lower and repeat pulling up to the right side of the bar.

NOTE
- Change grip with each set – for example – if left hand was forward previously, make the right hand the forward hand the next set.

79b. SELF-SPOTTING APPROACH

To assist in the development of performing a close grip pull-up, a bench is placed under the feet. With arms extended holding your bodyweight, position one foot on the bench provided. In raising the body, keeping the tension on the arms – slowly add the pressure of the foot to the bench to assist in raising the body.

79b. STARTING POSITION

MIDPOINT –
Raise body with leg assistance

NOTE
- Focus on the tension on the arms with the assistance of the leg being secondary.
- This approach helps maintain good posture (form), build strength and confidence.
- Over time as you become stronger the assistance of the leg is reduced or removed from the exercise.
- Change forward grip with each set to target different regions.

THE BODY COACH

Exercise 80 – Cable Pull-Downs

Target Area(s): Back, arms and abdominal muscles.
Equipment: Cable (or resistance band)

STARTING POSITION   MIDPOINT

INSTRUCTION
- Stand facing lat pull-down or high pulley cable machine.
- Grip bar with palms facing down.
- Activate abdominal brace and focus on deep breathing.
- Breathing out, pull bar down forward of the body towards the hips, maintaining a slight bend in the elbow as you pull down.
- Breathe in and control bar back up to starting point.

NOTE
- Ensure head and neck alignment is maintained at all times with the rest of the body for the development of good posture.
- This exercise can be performed with a close-grip, natural shoulder-width or wide grip position in a kneeling or standing position.

Exercise 81 – Medicine Ball Throw Downs

Target Area(s): Back, arms and abdominal muscles (power).
Equipment: Medicine Ball

START

SIMULTANEOUSLY THRUST ARMS DOWN AND JUMP

INSTRUCTION
- Stand tall, brace abdominals and extend Rebound Medicine Ball™ overhead with arms straight.
- Simultaneously activate abdominal muscles whilst thrusting Medicine Ball downwards to ground (advanced athletes only).
- Upon landing bend legs slightly to absorb shock through body.
- Catch ball after it bounces. Reset body position and repeat.
- This exercise is a power based exercise.
- Ensure ball is thrust slightly forward of body.

VARIATIONS
- Jump, dish body, thrust down.
- Overhead throws (soccer throw-ins).
- In starting position with Medicine Ball above head, time how long it takes to complete five thrust downs.
  (Time = seconds)

THE BODY COACH

BACK & ARM STRENGTHENING EXERCISES

71. Weighted Arm Extension

Perform__sets,__reps

72a. Prone Upper Back Drills

Perform__sets,__reps

72b. Prone Upper Back Drills

Perform__sets,__reps

72c. Fitness Ball Reverse Flyes

Perform__sets,__reps

73. Single Arm Pull Downs

Perform__sets,__reps

74a. Double Arms Pull Downs

Perform__sets,__reps

74b. Double Arms Pull Downs

Perform__sets,__reps

74c. Double Arms Pull Downs

Perform__sets,__reps

75. Wide Grip Pull-ups: 45-degrees

Perform__sets,__reps

76. Supine Biceps Pull-ups: 45-degrees   **77a. Reverse Grip Chin-ups**   **77b. Reverse Grip Chin-ups - Assisted**

Perform__sets,__reps   Perform__sets,__reps   Perform__sets,__reps

78a. Wide Grip Chin-ups   **78b. Wide Grip Chin-ups - Assisted**   **79a. Close Grip Pull-ups**

Perform__sets,__reps   Perform__sets,__reps   Perform__sets,__reps

79b. Close Grip Pull-ups - Assisted   **80. Cable Pull Downs**   **81. Medicine Ball Throw Downs**

Perform__sets,__reps   Perform__sets,__reps   Perform__sets,__reps

NOTE
- Perform exercises using opposite arms or leg, if required
- Refer to chapter 9 for establishing repetitions (reps) and sets

Chapter 7

Chest and Arm Muscles

Strengthening the chest and arms in unison with the abdominal region plays a major role in body balance between the upper and lower body. The basic rule for all push-up exercises is the narrower the hand position, the greater the triceps contribution and the lesser the chest contribution; conversely, the wider the hand position, the greater the chest contribution and the lesser the triceps contribution. Most importantly, ensure the head and neck is aligned and maintained with a strong abdominal brace and neutral spine position at all times with the rest of the body for the development of good posture. Start by building strength with arms close to the body when lowering and raising the body. Master the close-grip push-up in a modified position, then kneeling and on toes before moving to wider hand position. The primary muscles targeted in this chapter are:

- **Pectoralis (Chest) Region** – Large fan-shaped muscle that covers the front of the upper chest. Exercises include bar dips and push-up variations.

- **Triceps** – The back of the upper arm. Exercises include pushing movements like close grip push-ups and arm dips, as follows.

THE BODY COACH

PUSH-UP VARIATIONS

Exercise 82 – Modified Push-Up Series

Target Area(s): Chest, arms (triceps), serratus anterior and abdominal muscles.

Objective: Modified push-ups allow endurance of the chest, arms, serratus and abdominal to occur by decreasing the intensity of the push-up exercises through lever length or decline angle of body. As the body angle goes lower to the ground and/or lever length increases, the intensity of the exercise also increases. In saying this, it is important that in the initial development of core strength that modified push-ups are mastered and strength endurance obtained (i.e. 30-60 seconds of continuous push-ups without losing form. Start with close-grip position in all three positions described until stronger, before widening grip or performing exercises with hands on ground.

82a: STARTING POSITION   MIDPOINT

82a: Short lever, low-intensity push-up exercise – Kneeling with hands resting on solid foundation such as a chair or bench. Keep arms against the body when lowering and raising the body – focusing on building muscle endurance as well as head being well forward of the hands.

82b: STARTING POSITION   MIDPOINT

82b: Long lever, low-intensity push-up exercise – Stand with hands resting forward on solid foundation at approximately waist height, such as the rear of a solid chair, table or kitchen bench. Exercising at this level can help you achieve good posture and muscle endurance and is a good starting point for the beginner or athletes involved in endurance sports using the upper body such as swimming.

82c. STARTING POSITION   MIDPOINT

82c: Long lever, moderate to high intensity exercise – Stand with hands resting forward on solid foundation (bench or chair) at knee height.

THE BODY COACH

INSTRUCTION

- Kneel (or stand) on floor in front of raised solid foundation (i.e. table, bench or chair).
- Rest hands shoulder-width apart and turn elbow crease forwards to allow the upper arm to slide against the body when lowering and raising.
- Breathe in as you lower the body until the chest just touches the bench, ensuring head is well forward of the bench.
- Breathe out as you push up to the starting position.
- Maintain a tight body (strong abdominal brace to avoid lower back arching) from the shoulder to the knee throughout the movement and keep upper part of arm in contact with body (Close-Grip Push-Up) when lowering and raising.

NOTE

- Only widen handgrip placement once strength endurance has been achieved with close-grip variations, as this forms part of the core-strength continuum.
- Ensure head and neck alignment is maintained at all times with the rest of the body for the development of good posture.
- The goal is to progressively improve time performing a set of push-ups (i.e. 30 or 60 seconds continuous) without losing form or technique. This builds essential endurance that enables one to increase the intensity of the push-up exercise on the ground found in exercise 83 and 84.
- In breathing, breathe out as you exert a force (i.e. push-up or straighten the arms) and breathe in as you recover (i.e. lower the body or bend the arms).

Exercise 83 – Kneeling Push-Up

Target Area(s): Chest, arms (triceps) and abdominal muscles.

STARTING POSITION   MIDPOINT

INSTRUCTION
- Kneel on floor in a front support position with hands shoulder-width apart and eye line forwards over fingernails.
- Breathe in as you lower the body until the chest lowers near the floor.
- Then breathe out as you push-up to the starting position.
- Maintain a tight body from the shoulders to the knee.
- Ensure head and neck alignment is maintained at all times with the rest of the body for the development of good posture.

HAND PLACEMENT VARIATIONS
- **Close-grip** – hands positioned directly under shoulders with upper arm sliding against body when lowering and raising (master this exercise before progressing).
- **Normal position** – hands positioned outside shoulder alignment.
- **Wide grip** – hands wide.
- **Split grip** – one hand forward of shoulder the other hand back.

THE BODY COACH

Exercise 84 – Push-Up Variations (a-d)

Target Area(s): Chest, arms (triceps) and abdominal muscles.

84a. STARTING POSITION **MIDPOINT**

INSTRUCTION
84a.   CLOSE-GRIP
- Start in a front support position – hands under shoulders, body leaning slightly forward with eye line directly over fingernails and abdominal muscles braced.
- Breathing in, bend at the elbows and slowly lower the body towards the ground.
- Keeping the arms close to the body, breathe out as you straighten the arms.

NOTE
- Ensure neutral spine position is maintained from strong abdominal brace to avoid lower back sagging.
- Also ensure head and neck alignment is maintained at all times with the rest of the body for the development of good posture.

VARIATION
- Introduce unstable surface such as a Medicine Ball, Fitness Ball or Wobble Board to increase the challenge as strength levels are improved.

84b.　NORMAL GRIP
- Hands outside shoulder alignment.

84c.　WIDE GRIP
- Hands wider than shoulder-width.

84d: SPLIT GRIP
- One hand forward the other back.

- Reverse hands each set for muscle balance.

NOTE
- Only progress through exercises (84b-d) once Exercise 84a has been mastered – strength, endurance and coordination.

Exercise 85 – Medicine Ball Push-Up (a-b)

Target Area(s): Chest, arms (triceps) and abdominal muscles.
Equipment: Medicine Ball

85a. STARTING POSITION   **MIDPOINT**

85b. LEVEL 2:
ON TOES TO INCREASE EXERCISE
INTENSITY   **MIDPOINT**

INSTRUCTION
- Lie on Medicine Ball and place hands on top side with thumbs facing forward.
- 85a. kneeling.
- 85b. on toes.
- Breathing out, raise the body up to an extended position.
- Breathe in and lower body.

NOTE
- Maintain a tight body position throughout movement.
- Keep head in neutral position aligned with body at all times for the development of good posture and technique.

Exercise 86 – Fitness Ball Push-Up: Hands on Ball

Target Area(s): Chest, arms (triceps) and abdominal muscles.
Equipment: Fitness Ball

STARTING POSITION

MIDPOINT

INSTRUCTION
- Lie on Fitness Ball and place hands on top side of ball.
- Breathing out, raise the body up to an extended position.
- Breathe in and lower body.

NOTE
- Maintain a tight body position throughout movement.
- Ensure head and neck alignment is also maintained at all times with the rest of the body for the development of good posture and technique.

VARIATION
- **RAISE ONE FOOT OFF GROUND** – lower and raise body ensuring strong abdominal brace. Have coach support you whilst performing this exercise.

THE BODY COACH

Exercise 87 – Fitness Ball Push-Up: Feet on Ball (a-c)

Target Area(s): Chest, arms (triceps) and abdominal muscles.
Equipment: Fitness Ball

STARTING POSITION   MIDPOINT

INSTRUCTION
- Walk out and place hands in front support position with eye line over fingernails and shins (or feet) resting on ball.
- To reduce wrist stress, clench fist and rest on knuckles (as shown).
- Breathing out, raise the body up to an extended position.
- Breathe in and lower body.
- Maintain a tight body position (dish abdominal contraction) throughout movement.

MODIFICATION

- **87b. SHORT LEVER** – resting on the ball across one's thighs decreases the intensity of the exercise, by increasing the base of support and shortening the lever length.

- **87c. LONG LEVER** – resting on the ball on your shin or ankle area and even more extreme on your toes increases the intensity of the exercise by increasing the lever length and reducing the base of support.

87b. SHORT LEVER – thighs or knee   87c. LONG LEVER (on toes)

NOTE

- Ensure good head and neck alignment and neutral spine position is maintained at all times for the development of good posture and technique.

Exercise 88 – Bench Arm Dips (a-b)

Target Area(s): Arms (triceps).
Equipment: Chair (or bench)

88a. STARTING POSITION

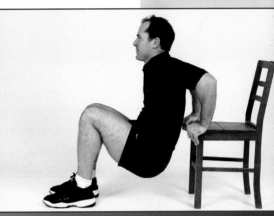

MIDPOINT

INSTRUCTION
- Sit on edge of solid chair or bench and place hands by your side with fingers facing forward.
- Step slightly forward with your body away from seat or bench with legs at 90 degrees.
- Bracing the abdominal muscles, breathe in as you bend your arms and lower your body until arms bent at 90-degrees.
- Breathe out as you rise up to straighten your arms.

NOTE
- Keep arms close to the body when lowering and raising

88b. LEG RAISED (Increases Intensity)

Extend one leg out in front of you and hold whilst performing the bench arm dip exercise.

Exercise 89 – Bar Dips (a-b)

Target Area(s): Chest and Arms (triceps).
Equipment: Parallel Bars (and bench)

INSTRUCTION

- Rise up onto parallel bars and extend arms.
- Ensure shoulders and head are kept high to avoid sinking and good body position is maintained.
- Breathe in and lower the body, leaning the chest slightly forward until the arms reach 90 degree angle (no lower).
- Breathe out and raise body, keeping the arms close to body.

89a. STARTING POSITION　　　　　　　　**MIDPOINT**

THE BODY COACH

MODIFICATIONS

89b. FOOT SUPPORT

Place one foot up on a bench to help support the lift of the body and maintain good body alignment. Depending on the athlete's ability level, promote the use of the leg when performing the bar dip until good strength endurance is achieved. Decrease use of the leg as the athlete becomes stronger.

NOTE
- Focus on the tension on the arms with the assistance of the leg being secondary.
- This approach helps maintain good posture (form), build strength and confidence.
- Over time as you become stronger the assistance of the leg is reduced or removed from the exercise.

89b. STARTING POSITION   MIDPOINT

CHEST & ARM STRENGTHENING EXERCISES

82a. Modified Push-up – kneeling

Perform__sets,__reps

82b. Modified Push-up

Perform__sets,__reps

82c. Modified Push-up

Perform__sets,__reps

83. Kneeling Modified Push-up

Perform__sets,__reps

84. Push-up

Perform__sets,__reps

85a. Medicine Ball Push-up: Kneeling

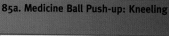

Perform__sets,__reps

85b. Medicine Ball Push-up: Toes

Perform__sets,__reps

86. Fitness Ball Push-up – Hands on Ball

Perform__sets,__reps

87a. Fitness Ball Push-up - Feet on Ball

Perform__sets,__reps

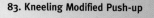

THE BODY COACH

87b. Fitness Ball Push-up - Short Lever | **87c. Fitness Ball Push-up - Long Lever** | **88a. Bench Dips**

Perform__sets,__reps   Perform__sets,__reps   Perform__sets,__reps

88b. Bench Dips – Leg Extended | **89a. Bar Dips** | **89b. Bar Dips - Assisted**

Perform__sets,__reps   Perform__sets,__reps   Perform__sets,__reps

NOTE: Refer to chapter 9 for establishing repetitions (reps) and sets.

Chapter 8

Shoulder and Rotator Cuff Strength

The shoulder joint is a ball and socket joint formed by three bones known as the clavicle, scapula and humerus. The most freely moving joint in the body, the shoulder is dependant on the muscles and ligaments surrounding the joint to stabilize it.

The best way to strengthen the deep shoulder (rotator cuff) muscles and prevent shoulder injuries is with resistance band exercises. Prior to starting any exercise routine always gain approval by your doctor and guidance from a physiotherapist in relation to what exercises are best for you as well as appropriate reps and sets. Any person who suffers a shoulder injury, tension or pain should always seek proper medical advice.

SHOULDER STRENGTHENING EXERCISES – Rotator Cuff

Selected exercises to be approved by your doctor

1. EXTERNAL ROTATION

Attach tubing to door handle, pole or chair. Stand with furthest arm away to be exercised. Bend elbow at 90 degrees and grasp tubing. Rotate arm away from your body and slowly return arm to starting position. Repeat on opposite arm, if necessary.

Perform__sets,__reps,__times daily

2. INTERNAL ROTATION

Attach tubing to door handle, pole or chair. Stand with closest arm to be exercised toward band. Bend elbow at 90 degrees and grasp tubing. Rotate arm in towards your body and slowly return arm to starting position. Repeat on opposite arm, if necessary.

Perform__sets,__reps,__times daily

3. ADDUCTION

Attach tubing to door handle, pole or chair. Stand with closest arm to be exercised toward tubing. Hold tubing in hand and pull directly across body and slowly return arm to starting position. Repeat on opposite arm, if necessary.

Perform__sets,__reps,__times daily

4. EXTENSION – STANDING

Attach tubing to door handle, pole or chair. Stand facing toward tubing, holding it in one hand. Pull tubing directly behind you and slowly return arm to starting position. Repeat on opposite arm, if necessary.

Perform__sets,__reps,__times daily

THE BODY COACH

5. FLEXION – SINGLE ARM

Stand with tubing supported under foot. Hold opposite end in hand and pull arm directly out to the front of your body and slowly return arm to starting position. Repeat on opposite arm, if necessary.

Note: For true abduction extend arms directly to the side of body.

Perform__sets,__reps,__times daily

6. ABDUCTION 30 DEGREES

Stand with tubing supported under foot in the middle. Hold opposite end in hand and pull arm directly out 30 degrees forward of lateral and slowly return arm to starting position.

Perform__sets,__reps,__times daily

7. HORIZONTAL ABDUCTION

Lie on bench or across chair with tubing attached directly under shoulder level. Grip tubing and pull arm straight out from your body until 90 degrees at shoulder level. Slowly return arm to starting position. Repeat on opposite arm, if necessary.

Perform__sets,__reps,__times daily

Chapter 9

Core Strength Training Routines

Core strength is a long-term project. Think of it like the steps for renovating a house – some areas need to be rebuilt and other areas simply maintained. To get where you want to go you need a plan. This plan needs to be monitored and assessed regularly and adjusted appropriately to suit ever-changing needs. Some areas may require a lot more attention than others to rebuild balance in the form of strength, endurance, stability, mobility, flexibility, pliability or coordination. The Core Strength Basics approach is based on building muscle synergy throughout the whole body that will ultimately make it work more efficiently over longer periods of time. In most cases, this involves going back to basics applying low-level intensity exercises, building muscle endurance and then progressing from here.

Starting out too hard too early can place too much stress on already overloaded muscles, unstable or hypermobile joints. Each exercise therefore serves as a test (specific tests in chapter 10). Appropriate core strength can be gauged by the ability of the athlete to maintain a good body position whilst applying the 3B's Principle™.

Training Schedule

Beginners should work the whole body at least 3 days per week for around 30 minutes, with one rest day between workouts. For example: Monday, Wednesday and Friday. This is important as your muscles rebuild whilst resting. As you progress towards **Intermediate** and **Advanced** levels, you want to add more exercises to your routine to increase the overload, but target only specific muscle groups. This is called split training, where you might train the upper body 3 days a week and the lower body 3 days a week, including the abdominal muscles. Spreading your workouts over several days will generally decrease the length of each training session, but in turn makes it possible to train at a higher intensity through more exercises being performed targeting one specific muscle group.

There are a number of training splits that can be developed, including 4, 5 and 6-day routines that rotate between various muscle groups. The **upper body** includes the chest, back, shoulders and arms (biceps and triceps). Whereas the **lower body** targets the abdominal muscles, lower back, buttocks and leg muscles. For instance, an intermediate level trainer performing a 6-day split may work chest, shoulders and triceps on Monday's and Friday's upper body split and back and biceps on Wednesday's upper body split. A similar breakdown of muscle groups can be made with the lower body region. The following table provides an example training schedule:

LEVEL	Split	Mon	Tue	Wed	Thu	Fri	Sat	Sun
Beginner								
Whole Body	**None**	Whole Body	Rest	Whole Body	Rest	Whole Body	Rest	Rest
Intermediate								
Each body part 3 days a week	6-Day	Upper Body	Lower Body	Upper Body	Lower Body	Upper Body	Lower Body	Rest
Advanced								
Upper and lower body 2 days each	4-Day	Upper Body	Lower Body	Rest	Upper Body	Lower Body	Rest	Rest

Determining Repetitions and Sets

The ideal number of repetitions (reps) varies between 8-12 and 12-15 reps, for strength and endurance respectively, and 3 sets per exercise. As muscle needs to be overloaded to stimulate growth, in body weight training this is achieved through a core strength continuum. In lifting weights you simply add more weight to the bar, whereas in body weight training you can increase the intensity or overload by slowing down the time it takes to perform each repetition (i.e. from 2 seconds to 4 seconds), otherwise performing a more challenging exercise for the same muscle group – the goal of the core strength continuum. As one exercise becomes easy, you move up the core strength continuum to a harder exercise of the same muscle group. This may entail going from performing a push-up on the ground to having the feet resting on a fitness ball to increase the challenge. In other cases, it may require starting with harder exercises first and easy exercises later in the training so you fall within this 8–12 repetition range as the exercises are much harder to perform from fatigue.

Overload in bodyweight training can also come from rotating exercises and reducing the rest periods between sets. Time on task can also be used as a replacement of repetitions. As not one routine one fits all, having various options available provides the variety required to achieve your goal. Ultimately it becomes a game of trial and error, as some participants will easily surpass the set amount of reps, where others fail. So, aim for the 8–12 repetition range. If you do it easy, change the exercise or simply slow the exercise down so you spend more time under tension. For example, if you can do 12 push-ups easy in 12 seconds, slow it down to perform up to 12 reps in 24 or 36 seconds (2 or 3 seconds each rep) maintaining good form and you will be challenged. (Refer to page 14 for further details on time under tension). Ultimately, the variations supplied above will help establish the repetitions and sets to suit your needs for overloading a muscle group for optimal strength gains between muscle groups. Vary exercises regularly to maintain this challenge and always focus on improving the link between weaker and more dominant muscle groups throughout the body for better movement synergy.

Recovery or Rest Periods

Allowing 30–180 seconds recovery is recommended between most exercises, if working the same muscle group or the same exercise is being repeated. Recovery is generally based on two key elements:
1 Purpose of your training – low, medium or high intensity (endurance, strength or power based).
2 One's current fitness or strength level.
The longer the recovery period the fresher you will be – choose accordingly.

Joint Actions or Articulations

Focusing on the angle of which a joint is strengthened helps maintain muscular balance. For instance, strengthening the back muscles requires multiple angular motions involving the arms, shoulder joint and scapula demonstrated by the following three example exercises – pull-ups, chin-ups and pull downs. In these three exercises, the angle of pull differs yet similar muscles are targeted. Joint actions or articulations (angles) need to be taken into consideration to ensure muscular balance at each joint around the body.

Three examples of working the back muscles through different joint angles include:

1. PULL-UPS   **2. CHIN-UPS**   **3. PULL-DOWNS**

THE BODY COACH

10 Key Points of Core Strength Training

The initial emphasis of all exercise must be placed on building muscle endurance in pull, push and static exercises. Focus should be placed on strengthening from the inside out to build a strong core that will hold a better body position or posture for longer periods of time in training. Once a good endurance base is acquired, the exercise intensity can be increased. This is achieved by increasing the lever length, exercise angle, activity, resistance or bodyweight load. In the meantime, the 10 key points for core strength improvements include:

1 Focus on static exercises, good body positioning and deep breathing as a prerequisite to developing good body awareness and better muscle control.
2 Focus first on obtaining general muscle endurance, for the whole body.
3 Ensure correct technique and form is maintained throughout.
4 Start with 10-20 minutes of exercise. Allow adequate rest between exercises of up to 30 seconds for a circuit format and between 30-180 seconds for more demanding exercises using the same muscle group.
5 Stretch in between sets to keep muscles pliable.
6 Think of exercises in terms of push, pull or static in nature with movement articulations at varying angles. All of which need to be strengthened to improve posture.
7 Test strengths and weaknesses every 4 weeks and make necessary adjustments of exercises, repetitions, sets and recovery.
8 Vary the location where you exercise (indoor/outdoor) for variety.
9 Plan your sessions ahead of time and be prepared (i.e. equipment).
10 Keep records of exercises, reps, sets and time so you can monitor your progress.

Stretching in between exercises is recommended, whereas, when an athlete is involved in a circuit type format moving from one exercise straight to the next or one muscle group to another, adapting a low-level intensity, a short rest period of only 15-30 seconds may apply.

Core Strength Continuum

The Core Strength Continuum provides the athlete and coach with a series of functional pathways that progress from basic level (Level 1) to more advanced movements (Levels 2 & 3) for each area of the body. As not one size fits all, variations and modifications of these exercises can be made to suit the athlete's specific progressive core strength requirements by working with a qualified health professional. Three levels are used as an example of the progression of coordination and intensity of an exercise. In the case of a push-up there are 20 or so progressions that can be used in order to perfect the movement. It is important to understand that body awareness and coordination are prerequisites for building strength. Accordingly, a number of Level 1 exercises are based on the concept of mastering the finer details of the movement and body position. If an athlete is unable to perform a particular exercise with good form for 12 repetitions, then the intensity of the exercise must be reduced by applying an easier exercise. This foundational approach forms part of the core strength continuum. The following example outlines the application of a core-strength continuum.

Core Strength Continuum

Level 1	Level 2	Level 3

PUSH-UP – PROGRESSION (ON KNEES)

Exercise 82b	Exercise 82c	Exercise 84a

THE BODY COACH

- The top row on the chart above progresses in coordination and intensity from left to the right – Level 1 to Level 3.
- The second row outlines the specific muscle group or area of the body targeted.
- The third row provides photograph of the drill and exercise number which can be referred to within the book.
- If an athlete is able to perform a particular exercise for 12 repetitions or more with good form, a new exercise may need to be introduced that challenges the athlete. Otherwise, slow each repetition down to increase the time under tension and exercise intensity.
- Go to page 186 to design your own core-strength continuum model.
- As an athlete or coach your goal is to progress through a core strength continuum relative to your ability levels, as what may seem hard for some is easy for others and visa-versa.

Core Strength Training Routine – Samples

The following pages outline core-strength routine samples that cover a whole range of sporting and lifestyle activities including:

- Post–Pregnancy
- Racquet and Bat Sports
- Balance Sports
- Golf

- Running
- Ball Sports
- Swimming
- Kids

Always warm-up and stretch the body before and after exercising. As not every routine will fit each individual, it is important to adapt the appropriate exercises and vary the exercises, sets and reps accordingly to suit your training needs under the guidance and supervision of a fitness and health professional.

Core Strength for Post-Pregnancy

Target Group: 4–8 weeks after child birth only after gaining your doctors approval

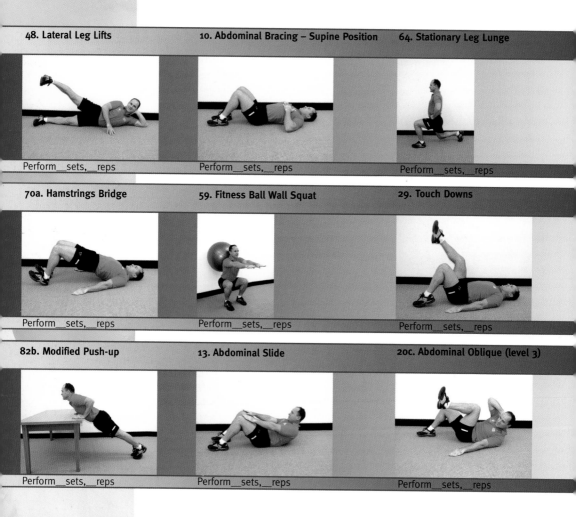

48. Lateral Leg Lifts

Perform__sets,__reps

10. Abdominal Bracing – Supine Position

Perform__sets,__reps

64. Stationary Leg Lunge

Perform__sets,__reps

70a. Hamstrings Bridge

Perform__sets,__reps

59. Fitness Ball Wall Squat

Perform__sets,__reps

29. Touch Downs

Perform__sets,__reps

82b. Modified Push-up

Perform__sets,__reps

13. Abdominal Slide

Perform__sets,__reps

20c. Abdominal Oblique (level 3)

Perform__sets,__reps

Core Strength for Running

Target Groups: All sports that involve running, speed and agility
Note: Regular stretching and massage is important for maintaining muscle pliability

48. Lateral Leg Lifts

Perform__sets,__reps

18. Medicine Ball Raise

Perform__sets,__reps

19. Lateral Side Raises

Perform__sets,__reps

33. Knee Raise

Perform__sets,__reps

70a. Hamstrings Bridge

Perform__sets,__reps

55. Resistance Band Kickbacks

Perform__sets,__reps

64. Stationary Leg Lunge

Perform__sets,__reps

69. Single Leg Bow

Perform__sets,__reps

63. Assisted Single Leg Squat

Perform__sets,__reps

57. Medicine Ball Leg Curls

Perform__sets,__reps

89a. Bar Dips

Perform__sets,__reps

45. Fitness Ball Ins-and-Outs

Perform__sets,__reps

Core Strength for Racquet & Bat Sports

Target Groups: Badminton, Baseball, Cricket, Hockey, Lacrosse, Softball, Squash, Tennis.
Note: Also use Core-Strength for Running and Resistance Band Exercises

Chapter 8 – Rotator Cuff Exercise Series

Perform__sets,__reps

75. Wide Grip Pull-ups: 45-degrees

Perform__sets,__reps

86. Fitness Ball Push-up – hands on ball

Perform__sets,__reps

89a. Bar Dips

Perform__sets,__reps

78a. Wide Grip Chin-ups

Perform__sets,__reps

8. Body Dish

Perform__sets,__reps

16c. Fitness Ball Abdominal Crunch (Level 3)

Perform__sets,__reps

22a. Fitness Ball Oblique Twist

Perform__sets,__reps

20e. Abdominal Oblique (level 5)

Perform__sets,__reps

59. Fitness Ball Wall Squat

Perform__sets,__reps

70a. Hamstrings Bridge

Perform__sets,__reps

66. Multi-directional Lunges

Perform__sets,__reps

THE BODY COACH

Core Strength for Ball Sports

Target Groups: Basketball, Handball, Netball, Volleyball, Waterpolo (see swimming)

Note: See 'Core-Strength for Running' drills for additional exercises

Chapter 8 – Rotator Cuff Exercise Series	52. Pelvic Lifts	33. Knee Raise
Perform__sets,__reps	Perform__sets,__reps	Perform__sets,__reps
85b. Medicine Ball Push-up: Toes	78a. Wide Grip Chin-ups	89a. Bar Dips
Perform__sets,__reps	Perform__sets,__reps	Perform__sets,__reps
16c. Fitness Ball Abdominal Crunch (Level 3)	22a. Fitness Ball Oblique Twist	23. Fitness Ball Prone Roll-out
Perform__sets,__reps	Perform__sets,__reps	Perform__sets,__reps
7. Level 2. Fitness Ball Isometric Rear Supports	59. Fitness Ball Wall Squat	66. Multi-directional Lunges
Perform__sets,__reps	Perform__sets,__reps	Perform__sets,__reps

Core Strength for Balance Sports

Target Groups: Cycling, Ice-skating, Skateboarding, Snow-Boarding, Snow-Skiing, Surfing, Wakeboarding, Water-skiing.

48. Lateral Leg Lifts

Perform__sets,__reps

70a. Hamstrings Bridge

Perform__sets,__reps

7. Level 2. Fitness Ball Isometric Rear Supports

Perform__sets,__reps

33. Knee Raise

Perform__sets,__reps

26a. Collins Lateral Fly™ Series (Level 3)

Perform__sets,__reps

16c. Fitness Ball Abdominal Crunch (Level 3)

Perform__sets,__reps

69. Single Leg Bow

Perform__sets,__reps

63. Assisted Single Leg Squat

Perform__sets,__reps

89a. Bar Dips

Perform__sets,__reps

77a. Reverse Grip Chin-ups

Perform__sets,__reps

45. Fitness Ball Ins-and-Outs

Perform__sets,__reps

20d. Abdominal Oblique (level 4)

Perform__sets,__reps

THE BODY COACH

Core Strength for Swimming

Target Groups: Swimming, Water polo, Surfing, Diving
Note: Regular stretching and massage is important for maintaining muscle pliability

48. Lateral Leg Lifts	7. Level 2. Fitness Ball Isometric Rear Supports	25b. Collins Lateral Fly™ Series (Level 2)

Perform__sets,__reps	Perform__sets,__reps	Perform__sets,__reps

33. Knee Raise	16d. Fitness Ball Abdominal Crunch (Level 4)	19. Lateral Side Raises

Perform__sets,__reps	Perform__sets,__reps	Perform__sets,__reps

59. Fitness Ball Wall Squat	82c. Modified Push-up	89a. Bar Dips
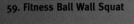		
Perform__sets,__reps	Perform__sets,__reps	Perform__sets,__reps

75. Wide Grip Pull-ups: 45-degrees	80. Cable Pull Downs	8. Body Dish

Perform__sets,__reps	Perform__sets,__reps	Perform__sets,__reps

Core Strength for Golf

Target Group: Golf

Note: Regular stretching and massage is important for maintaining muscle pliability

Chapter 8 – Rotator Cuff Exercise Series	82c. Modified Push-up	75. Wide Grip Pull-ups: 45-degrees
Perform__sets,__reps	Perform__sets,__reps	Perform__sets,__reps
13. Abdominal Slide	**77a. Reverse Grip Chin-ups**	**22a. Fitness Ball Oblique Twist**
Perform__sets,__reps	Perform__sets,__reps	Perform__sets,__reps
28. Reverse Curls	**69. Single Leg Bow**	**20d. Abdominal Oblique (level 4)**
Perform__sets,__reps	Perform__sets,__reps	Perform__sets,__reps
58a. Body Weight Squat	**8. Body Dish**	**64. Stationary Leg Lunge**
Perform__sets,__reps	Perform__sets,__reps	Perform__sets,__reps

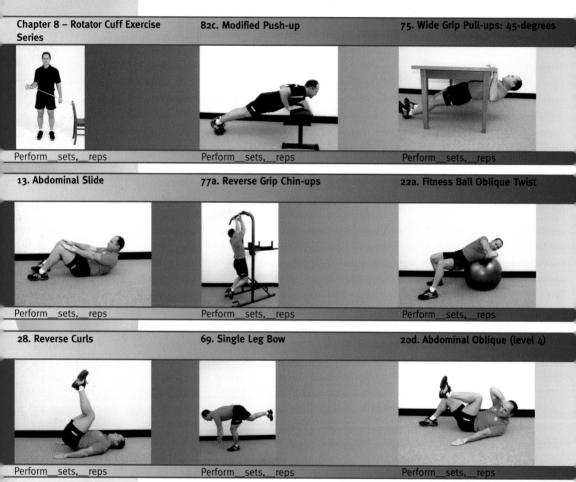

Core Strength for Kids

Target Group: Kids 8 years and older under direct supervision of coach or teacher

68. Skipping

Perform__sets,__reps

83. Kneeling Modified Push-up

Perform__sets,__reps

77a. Reverse Grip Chin-ups

Perform__sets,__reps

47. Wall-sits

Perform__sets,__reps

13. Abdominal Slide

Perform__sets,__reps

1a. Front Support Holds

Perform__sets,__reps

8. Body Dish

Perform__sets,__reps

28. Reverse Curls

Perform__sets,__reps

58a. Body Weight Squat

Perform__sets,__reps

69. Single Leg Bow

Perform__sets,__reps

64. Stationary Leg Lunge

Perform__sets,__reps

Design your own Core Strength Training Routine

Each sport or physical activity has its own unique requirements. With high intensity sports such as boxing, martial arts and judo you have the opportunity to work with your coach to set some goals and develop a training routine based upon the core strength continuum. With other sports such as horseback riding, show jumping, pistol shooting and even motor racing there are postural requirements that require a unique approach for more efficient body positioning. Which ever the case, after testing your core-body strength (see Chapter 10) and finding your strength and weaknesses visit each chapter and respective exercises for each muscle group to help design a program that brings back balance into your body and relative muscle synergy. The reps, sets, recovery and exercises need to be adjusted regularly to ensure a challenge is placed on the targeted muscle groups. Use the following chart to assist in designing your own core-strength training routine.

Core Strength Routine

Sport or Target Area:				
Exercise	Page No.	Reps	Sets	Recovery
1				
2				
3				
4				
5				
6				
7				
8				
9				
10				
11				
12				

Notes:

THE BODY COACH

Chapter 10

Testing Core Body Strength

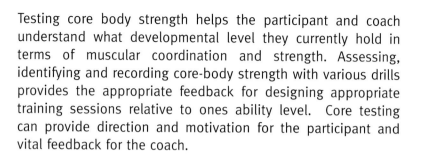

Testing core body strength helps the participant and coach understand what developmental level they currently hold in terms of muscular coordination and strength. Assessing, identifying and recording core-body strength with various drills provides the appropriate feedback for designing appropriate training sessions relative to ones ability level. Core testing can provide direction and motivation for the participant and vital feedback for the coach.

Maintaining excellent form and deep breathing is promoted over poor form. In the initial phases the major focus is on making small incremental improvements in body position of the athlete whilst combining core-stability and core-strength exercises adapting the core-strength continuum. Recording where one currently stands today needs to be broken down into two key elements:

1 **Quality of Movement** – how well the body is positioned, balanced, coordinated and/or readjusted throughout the movement; whether deep breathing pattern is maintained; correct tracking of the limbs and good movement rhythm and efficiency

2 **Number of Repetitions** – one can perform until loss of form

For instance, a squat exercise in core-strength training is focused primarily on the quality of movement as opposed to how many repetitions one can perform. On the other hand, a chin-up exercise working against gravity may focus primarily on the number of repetitions performed. Essentially, every core-strength exercise is a test – a test of quality of movement and strength. As a result, every core-strength exercise can be broken down into 5 key areas:

1 **Push Exercise** – eg. push-up
2 **Pull Exercise** – eg. chin-up
3 **Static Exercise** – eg. front support hold, chin-up hold, body dish
4 **Range of Motion** – eg. squat or lunge range of motion 'quality'

THE BODY COACH

5 Movement efficiency – visual assessment of athlete by the coach in terms of balance, coordination, timing, body mechanics, holding patterns, contraction, adjusting, breathing and muscular synergy whether in a static position or working through a range of motion.

The following tests help identifying any functional restrictions and other factors such as hypermobility and should be performed under the guidance of a qualified health or fitness professional after gaining your doctors approval.

CORE-STRENGTH TESTS

1. PUSH: The ability to perform a specific number of repetitions through a full range of movement without stopping or losing body position.

1a. Push-ups (see Ex. 82) | **1b. Bar Dips (see Ex. 87)**

Full push-up reps until fatigue or loss of form = _____

Full bar dip reps until fatigue or loss of form = _____

2. PULL: The ability to perform a specific number of repetitions through a full range of movement without stopping. Alternatively, being timed holding a 90 degree arm position on the chin-up bar.

2a. Wide-grip Chin-ups

2b. Reverse Grip Pull-ups

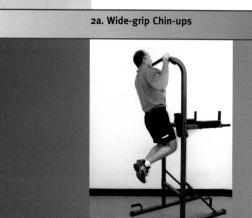

Full reps until fatigue or loss of form = _____   Full reps until fatigue or loss of form = _____

3. STATIC: The ability to hold a strong position without sagging, losing neutral spine or abdominal brace.

3a. Front Support Hold on Toes
3b. Front Support Hold – Feet on Ball

3c. Dish Hold – until loss of form

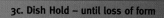

Seconds until fatigue or loss of form

3a = _____
3b = _____

(1) Seconds = _____
(2) Seconds = _____

THE BODY COACH

4. BODY MECHANICS: Assess the range of motion quality of the squat exercise. Aim to improve the quality of the movement and muscle coordination

Good form includes:
- Good muscle synergy and timing lowering to 90-degree leg angle
- Pelvis square
- Ear over shoulder, shoulder over knee, knee over toes (lateral view)
- Knees over toes (front view)
- Full range of movement with feet neutral and knees aligned over toes.
- Breathing in when lowering and out when rising

Poor form includes:
- Heels raise off ground
- Ankle and knees make first movement
- Knees forward of toes
- Leaning forward
- Body twisting
- Limited range
- Knees and/or feet roll inwards
- Lack of synergy
- Inability to lower legs to 90-degrees
- Holding breath
- Losing balance

In Summary

Essentially, all exercises can be used as a test of core body strength. Utilizing the 5 Key Areas in your approach allows you to identify weaknesses that may otherwise go unnoticed. It is often the finer details of one's body position and movement pattern that needs to be improved. This requires going back to basics and improving elements such as body awareness, balance and coordination, body positioning and alignment, breathing and proper range of motion. In some cases, it may require you to slow each movement down and in other cases have your body position readjusted by your coach. Either way, you have the opportunity to build your strongest body ever.

THE BODY COACH

For educational products go to:

International Managing Agent

Saxton Speakers Bureau (Australia)

- Website: www.saxton.com.au
- Email: speakers@saxton.com.au
- Phone: (03) 9811 3500
  International: +61 3 9811 3500

www.thebodycoach.com

Study in Australia

- International Fitness College for overseas students to study sport, fitness and personal training qualifications in Sydney Australia
- 3 month to 2 year student visa courses

www.sportandfitness.com.au

Core Strength Index

THE BODY COACH

Photo & Illustration Credits:

Cover Photo: getty-images, Germany
Cover Design: Jens Vogelsang
Photos: Paul Collins
Illustration p. 24: Svetlana Unger

Paul Collins
**Strength Training
for Women**

The combination of strength train-ing, aerobic exercise and healthy eating habits has proven to be most effective for fat loss and muscle toning. Strength Training for Women has been developed as a training guide as more women begin to understand the health benefits of this activity. A series of strength training routines for use in the gym as well as a body weight workout routine that can be performed at home are included.

About 144 pages, full-color print, 200 color photos
Paperback, $6^1/2''$ x $9^1/4''$
ISBN: 978-1-84126-248-2
$ 14.95 US
£ 9.95 UK / € 14.95

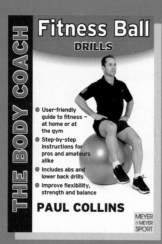

Paul Collins
Fitness Ball Drills

Fitness Ball Drills is a user-friendly exercise guide for achieving a stronger, leaner and more flexible body. The Fitness Ball is one of the most utilized pieces of gym and fitness equipment used throughout the world to tone, stretch and strengthen the whole body. Body Coach Paul Collins provides step-by-step coaching for improving posture, balance, coordination, strength and flexibility with more than 50 exercises that can easiliy be carried out at home or in the gym.

144 pages, full-color print
182 color photos
Paperback, $6^1/2''$ x $9^1/4''$
ISBN: 978-1-84126-221-5
$ 14.95 US
£ 9.95 UK / € 14.95

Paul Collins
Stretching Basics

Stretching Basics provides an introductory guide for stretching and flexibility exercises for sport, lifestyle, and injury prevention. Body Coach Paul Collins provides step-by-step instructions for more then 50 exercises meant to improve flexbility and range of motion, as well as to reduce muscular tension throughout the whole body. Stretching Basics is ideal for all age groups and ability levels.

144 pages, full-color print
255 color photos
Paperback, $6^1/2''$ x $9^1/4''$
ISBN: 978-1-84126-220-8
$ 14.95 US
£ 9.95 UK / € 14.95

www.m-m-sports.com

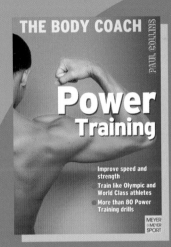

Paul Collins
Power Training

For many years, coaches and athletes have sought to improve power, a combination of speed and strength, in order to enhance performance. Power Training is designed as an educational tool to assist in the development of training programs that aim to keep athletes fit, strong and powerful all year round. 80 power training drills, tests and training routines are included which have also been used by Olympic and world class athletes to improve their performance. Power Training is an excellent guide for conditioned athletes.

136 pages, full-color print
247 photos
Paperback, $6^{1}/2$" x $9^{1}/4$"
ISBN: 978-1-84126-233-8
$ 14.95 US
£ 9.95 UK / € 14.95

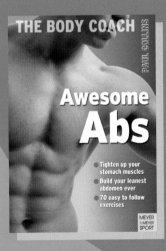

Paul Collins
Awesome Abs

The abdominal muscles serve a critical function in daily movement, sport and physical activity. A strong midsection helps support and protect your lower back region from injury. Better Abs for All is packed with over 70 easy-to-follow exercises and tests aimed at achieving a leaner abdomen, a stronger lower back, better posture and a trimmer waistline. You'll not only look and feel better, but athletes will find that a well-conditioned midsection allows them to change direction faster, generate force quicker and absorb blows better.

136 pages, full-color print
229 photos & 4 illustrations
Paperback, $6^{1}/2$" x $9^{1}/4$"
ISBN: 978-1-84126-232-1
$ 14.95 US
£ 9.95 UK / € 14.95